A Memoir

MEASURE

A Memoir

OF A MAN

FROM AUSCHWITZ SURVIVOR
TO PRESIDENTS' TAILOR

MARTIN GREENFIELD

WITH WYNTON HALL

REGNERY
PUBLISHING
A Salem Communications Company

Cataloging-in-Publication data on file with the Library of Congress
ISBN 978-1-62157-266-4

Published in the United States by
Regnery Publishing
A Salem Communications Company
300 New Jersey Ave NW
Washington, DC 20001
www.Regnery.com

Manufactured in the United States of America

10 9 8 7 6 5 4 3 2 1

Books are available in quantity for promotional or premium use. For information on discounts and terms, please visit our website: www.Regnery.com.

Distributed to the trade by
Perseus Distribution
250 West 57th Street
New York, NY 10107

CONTENTS

For the family I lost and love.

ברוך הוא שנותן חיים למתים

(BLESSED BE HE WHO GIVES LIFE TO THE DEAD.)

CHAPTER ONE

MEETING MENGELE

They say a man's shoes are the first thing a person notices.

I can still see his in my mind. Leather boots, dark like night, shining like mirrors. I'd never seen such shoes. In the tiny town of Pavlovo, Czechoslovakia, where I grew up, everyone had a farm, so boots were worn. But not shiny boots, not like these.

Shooting up and out the tops of his boots were billowy pants, no crease. His crisp shirt was tucked flat under his belt. A tightly tailored jacket covered in shiny buttons and pins drew my eyes up to his dark, smoothed-back hair. His elegant, calm face framed the gleaming monocle in his eye.

I did not yet know that this was the man called the "Angel of Death." I did not know that Dr. Josef Mengele was the Nazi physician who performed amputations without anesthesia, plucked out and collected blue eyeballs, tossed live babies into crackling fires, and gave twin girls candies before shooting them in the neck and using their corpses for medical experimentation.

I knew none of these things. How could I know? I was a fifteen-year-old boy. All I knew, standing in that line at Auschwitz, was that my father, Joseph Grünfeld; my mother, Tzyvia; my sisters, Simcha and Rivka; my five-year-old baby brother, Sruel Baer; and I, Maximilian, were in trouble and far from home.

I will tell you how we ended up at Auschwitz. In April 1944, on the second day of Passover, the Germans and Hungarians sur-rounded the Jewish homes in our village and gave us an hour to pack whatever we could carry. We came out into the street, were marched six miles, packed into cattle cars, and transported on a train to Mukačevo (then in Hungary, now in southwestern Ukraine). Just that fast.

The train chugged for twelve miles until we arrived at Mukačevo. The worst part was the imagining, the not knowing. Sometimes, when I let myself go back to Mukačevo in my mind, I wonder what thoughts and feelings must have been pulsing through my parents. Did they know the fate about to befall us? Had they hatched a plan in case our family got separated? Were they putting on a brave face for Simcha, Rivka, Sruel Baer, and me? Or did they think our time in the ghetto would be temporary, that we would go home after the war?

So many questions I still have. So many things I cannot know.

When we got to Mukačevo, the Germans herded us into a big building that housed a brick factory. The Germans had built wooden barracks all around the structure. Our family was actually lucky to be inside, because other Jewish families had to stay in tents when the barracks were full.

Even though we were in the ghetto only about a month, I was always thinking about our beautiful town of Pavlovo. You never saw a happier town than Pavlovo. We lived in the sweeping Carpathian Mountains, just a few miles from the Hungarian border. The Grünfeld family was well known and respected. My grandfather, Abraham, built our village's only synagogue. The fifty or so Jewish families that worshipped there were like one big family. On *Shabbat* (the Sabbath) we all gathered together. Everyone brought fresh vegetables grown from his garden, homemade breads, plum brandy, and the choicest wines. We were a tightknit little town. It was a beautiful life.

Dad's job as an industrial engineer meant he traveled almost every week. Sometimes during school breaks he would take me with him. We would sleep in tents on the job site, fish in the streams, and eat in the fields with the workers. I treasured those trips.

With Dad gone a lot, childrearing was mostly left up to my mother. She raised us well. We had our own farm, cows, and chickens and workers to take care of our land. Everything was grown fresh. Everything was our own. We used lamps and stoves for light and heat. We spoke Yiddish in our home and learned Czech in our school. When the adults didn't want us to hear something, they spoke Hungarian.

We were Orthodox but not fanatical. My parents were not nearly as religious as my mother's parents, Geitel and Fischel Berger, who lived with us. When I was three, my mother took me to *heder* (religious school). Because I was the oldest, she wanted me to set a good example for my siblings. I wanted so much to be a good example to them.

But none of that meant anything now. All that was over and done. We were in the Mukačevo ghetto waiting and worrying. My father was appointed a ghetto leader. He made sure families stayed together and mouths were fed. He was even free to walk in and out of the ghetto gates. He could have fled but didn't.

No one inside the ghetto spoke of corpses and crematoria. If they thought such things, they did not speak of them, at least not to me or my brother and sisters.

Of course, already I knew the Nazis were bad. At Mukačevo I watched as three Gestapo officers wrestled my grandfather to the floor so a fourth could cut off his long, beautiful beard after he refused to shave it.

"No!" cried my grandfather. "That is my strength!"

Still, they cut it.

Such images from youth never leave the mind.

Time spent with Abraham was always an adventure. My grandfather was so big, so strong. He trained white Arabian horses. In the winter he'd hook the horses to a sleigh and pull me through the snow, the horse bells tinkling all the way. Other memories were not so idyllic. Like the time I hit my head on a stable beam while riding a horse. My grandfather bandaged my head, lifted me back on the horse, and folded my hands around the reins. It was his way of teaching me to overcome fear. Today when I see the scar in the mirror, it makes me smile.

My grandfather was brave. Once, a band of robbers had been preying on our village. When my grandfather was crossing a bridge, one of the robbers attacked him. Grandfather wrestled the man to the ground, clamped his teeth down on the robber's finger, and bit it off. He wanted them to know not to attack our family or village.

But in Mukačevo, Abraham's courage was useless against the Germans. Seeing him pinned to the ground, humiliated, the Gestapo crawling all over him and mocking his faith, I realized that my grandfather's might was no match for the force we were about to face. It was also my first of many lessons in religious hate. I could not understand the Nazi attitude. I still don't. Killing people because of their religion? It made no sense to me. When people don't think for themselves, horrible things happen. This I know.

Because my father was a ghetto leader, our family was put on the very last transport from Mukačevo to Auschwitz. We were not told where we were headed. I remember standing still and quiet inside the cattle car, my brother's small hand wrapped tight inside mine. We arrived in Auschwitz at night. The train creaked to a slow stop. We waited for the door to fling open, but it didn't. The people inside craned to look through the opening in the car. Hours passed. Left overnight, the occupants were forced to relieve themselves inside the cattle car. My family huddled together to stay warm and calm.

The next morning, rays from the sun pierced our car and warmed our bodies. Sunlight flooded our enclosure as the door unlatched and opened. I remember thinking at that moment that nothing bad could happen on a day as beautiful as this. My youthful optimism was unprepared for the reality we were about to step into.

We hopped down from our car, and gaunt, sullen prisoners hustled us away.

"Out! Out! Hurry! Hurry!" yelled the inmates.

We were told to leave behind our bags and any items of worth we brought and to join the herd ambling toward the gates. It was larceny on the grandest of scales. In an instant the Germans seized generations' worth of toil and striving. Although we didn't realize it then, Hitler's mass-killing machine had been designed for ruthless efficiency, extracting every ounce of value from every possession confiscated. Prisoners with gold fillings had their teeth yanked and put in buckets of acid to burn away the dross of skin and bone; the hair shorn from our heads was used to make delayed-action bombs—nothing wasted, everything exploited.

Standing there, shuffling forward, robbery was now the least of our worries. I was too short to see over the adults. But as we got closer to the front of the line, I could make out Mengele. He did not look like the monster he was. He was handsome, even.

With just a few families now in front of us, I did not know what to do or expect. Finally, it was our family's turn. Mother clasped Rivka's hand and held my baby brother tight in her other arm. Mengele stood before us, quiet and calm. He looked us down and up before silently motioning for Mother to put my brother down. Mengele wanted to send Mother to the right and Sruel Baer to the left. But Mother would not let go of my brother; she clenched him closer. This time Mengele commanded she let go. Mother refused. So, with a flippant shrug of his shoulders, Mengele pointed for Mother, my baby brother, my younger sister Rivka, and my grandparents to all go to the left. To avoid panic or an uprising, the

Germans calmly told us the separation would merely be temporary, that we would see one another and be reunited later inside.

We wouldn't.

"See you later," my mother said looking back at us over her shoulder.

"See you later," I said waving.

I did not know it then, but with a flick of his baton, Mengele had sealed our family's fate. That moment, standing there in the Auschwitz selection line, was the last time I ever saw my mother; my baby brother, Sruel Baer; or Rivka.

Mengele ordered Father, Simcha, and me to go to the right. I was glad we had Simcha with us. That is, until the men and women on the right were separated and Simcha was taken away from Dad and me. For the longest time, I could never understand why Mengele did not send her to the left to be burned. Now, however, I think I know the answer, and it haunts me: Simcha was a tall, beautiful girl with silky blond hair—one of Mengele's genetic obsessions. Inside the camp I heard stories about the things the Germans liked to do to young, pretty Jewish girls. But no brother can let such thoughts linger too long, so I hoped it was only a rumor.

With Simcha gone, it was just Dad and me. The men and boys were then taken to an area where we were told to strip naked. Our shoes and clothes were seized. They then shaved our heads and bodies before splashing a disinfectant on us that burned like hell.

I'm not certain, but I do not think my father wanted the Germans to know we were father and son. We did, however, stand together in the tattoo line. That is why the serial numbers put into our arms were in order. My father's was "A4405." Mine was "A4406." The "A" meant Auschwitz.

At least Dad and I are still together, I remember thinking. *At least Brother and Sister are with Mother, Grandfather, and Grandmother.*

But those thoughts ended as quickly as they began.

A few hours later, in a quiet moment, my father pulled me close and whispered.

"I'm going to talk to you very seriously," he said. "Together, we will never survive, because working together we will suffer one for the other. We will suffer double. We must separate."

"No!" I cried. "You cannot leave me!"

"You must listen!" he said sternly. "It is the only way."

I shook my head *no* as if to shake away his words. The thought of his leaving me made me dizzy. It was a level of panic only a child on the edge of abandonment can feel.

"On your own, you will survive," he said. "You are young and strong, and I know you will survive. If you survive by yourself, you must honor us by living, by not feeling sorry for us. That is what you must do."

Today I am grateful for those words. They echo in my heart even still. It is a cruel thing, feeling guilty for surviving. But my father erased any future guilt and replaced it with purpose. It was a gift only a father's wisdom could give. It gave me a reason to go forward, a reason to be. It does still.

But back then I was just a stubborn teenage boy, so I argued. A lot. Still, Dad would not give in. His mind was made up, his words rehearsed. Soon, very quickly, a flood of anger filled me, because boys do not know any other way to show sadness to their father. I knew he loved me, but I could not understand. That night, lying in the dark, his decision went through my heart like a spear. *How could he do this?* I thought. *How could he leave me alone in the world? In this hell?*

The next morning, the Germans gave us our work orders. It was our second day in the camp. The soldiers asked if we knew any trades, like masonry, carpentry, medicine—that kind of thing. I was not listening so well because I was still hurting about my father's decision to split us up. But the next thing I knew, Dad grabbed my wrist and thrust it into the air.

"A4406," he said. "He is a mechanic. Very skilled."

Dad was not lying. I was always good with my hands and had worked a few years in a mechanic's garage in Hungary. Here is how that happened. When I was about twelve years old, the Germans had begun occupying some of the towns surrounding ours. Closer and closer they came. Stories began to spread about Jewish boys being taken and forced to work in German labor camps. So my father decided to send me away to Hungary to live with his cousin in Budapest. I begged my father to let my older friend Yitzhak Mermelstein come with me. Yitzhak was poor, so my father agreed to cover the cost of his train ticket.

When my father's cousin arrived at the train station in Budapest, I could instantly tell things were not going to work out. I spoke Hungarian poorly, and my father's cousin seemed annoyed with having two teenage boys intrude on his family's lovely apartment. When it came time for dinner, Yitzhak and I were put in the kitchen at the maid's table. I was too headstrong to handle such rudeness. That night, speaking in Yiddish, I told Yitzhak not to unpack.

"Tonight we run away," I said.

"Where will we go?" he asked.

"What does it matter?" I said. "We cannot stay here. We will leave tonight and find a place to stay. In the morning we will find jobs. We will be okay."

There was a nervousness in Yitzhak. His eyes always seemed on the verge of tears, and for that reason I think he found comfort in my unearned confidence.

That night we sneaked out. No note; we just left.

Yitzhak and I roamed through the night not knowing the city or the language. It was foolish and dangerous, but what did we know? We were kids. We wandered the streets for over an hour before spotting a small building bathed in a shimmering red light. We walked toward it. Standing at the door I could see Yitzhak's hands trembling, so I did the knocking. The door was whisked open, and a beautiful older girl answered. She could tell we were too young to understand what this place was, or what she and the other girls inside did for a living: we were kids, not customers. She welcomed us in and asked if we were lost or in trouble. She was kind and sweet, like an older sister. The clacking sound of high heels descending the stairs filled the room as another beautiful, kind girl in a flowing dress swished down and joined us. That night the pretty girls let us stay in an extra room. The next morning they introduced us to men who were oddly eager to please the girls by offering us jobs.

My job was working as a grease monkey repairing cars. Yitzhak did carpentry and small home repairs. Given our youthful innocence and *naïveté,* it took us a few days to understand that our new "sisters" were prostitutes and that our "apartment" was actually a whorehouse. But it mattered little. The girls were so nice and nurturing. They helped Yitzhak and me with our Hungarian, bought us sodas and ice cream, and took us to the beach on Sundays.

For the next three years, we lived with our surrogate sisters and made enough money to feed ourselves and earn our keep in the brothel. Life was good. Even though the Jews in Budapest were required to wear large yellow Stars of David, no one knew us, so we never wore them. Still, I wondered if the same could be said for my family back home. Each week I wrote letters to Mother and Father. I told them that Yitzhak and I had moved, but I didn't exactly tell them we were living with courtesans.

Then one day while fixing a car motor, my right hand got caught and mangled. One of our sisters rushed me to the hospital. There, I decided to write my parents a letter. Not to tell them what happened or where I was, just to keep up my correspondence. My injury meant I could not write. I showed one of my sisters a letter I had written and asked her to mimic my handwriting. She took down my message and mailed the letter from the hospital.

The instant my father saw the unfamiliar handwriting, he knew something was wrong. He hopped on a train and tracked me down at the hospital. The worst part was that he had already

gone to the brothel using the return address from my letters. Someone there told him I had gotten my hand caught in a motor and
was at the hospital.

Standing there, silent and stern, my father did not speak to me.
He did not need to. His gaze cast more shame upon me than his
words ever could. I wanted him to know the girls were like our
sisters, loving and kind and helping us so much. But we never spoke
of it. Instead, he took me home.

When we got back to Pavlovo, my five-year-old baby brother
was hanging on me as if I were a hero. I'd been away for over half
his life and hardly knew him. I had lost touch with home.

The next morning, my father explained that Jewish boys and
men in nearby towns were being rounded up and taken. He and
my godfather decided we should run and hide deep in the woods.
I had just spent years in Budapest living a carefree life without
restrictions, without fears. Now, just hours after coming home, my
father was packing me up, arming me with a handgun, and taking
me out in the field to practice shooting.

"I'm not going!" I said.

"Yes, you must!" Father yelled.

"I will never do that! Whatever happens to you, I want it to
happen to me. You separated me from you in Budapest. I'm not
going!"

"Hush! You don't understand the danger. You will obey me!"

"I will not! Not unless you go with me," I said.

I loved my father. I had missed him terribly while I was away.
What was the point of being back in Pavlovo if I had to hide in the
forest like some wounded animal?

The Nazis made the decision for us. The next day, the Germans and Hungarians surrounded our home and took us away.

⁓

But even if all that had not happened, even if I had not learned mechanical skills in Budapest, sitting there inside Auschwitz, my father would have probably made something up and told the Germans I possessed a trade. It was all part of his plan. Above the gates at Auschwitz was a sign. It read *Arbeit macht frei* ("Work makes you free"). By volunteering my skills as a mechanic, my father protected me. It was his way of marking me for the Germans as a Jew whose skills they could exploit, as one not to be burned.

As soon as my father offered up my skills, two Germans walked toward us to take me away. I then did something I should not have done, something stupid.

I ran.

Why, I do not know. Fences and soldiers were everywhere. Where did I think I was going? I cannot say. But for whatever reason, I ran.

A few paces into my sprint, I heard a barking German shepherd barreling down on me. My arms pumped hard as I stretched my stride and ran faster than I'd ever run before. The barks got louder. I snapped my head back over my shoulder and saw the dog closing in. He leapt and latched his teeth onto my leg. I looked down. The dog hung from my calf. I shoved his head with both hands. He snarled and gnashed violently as I struggled to pry him loose. The dog's jaw unlocked, taking a meaty chunk with him. Blood spurted on my prisoner uniform, the dog's mouth—everywhere. I tried not to cry. Not in front of my father, not in front of the other men and boys.

The two soldiers tromped over to retrieve the dog and make sure he was uninjured. They then snatched me up off the ground and hauled me away from the group. I thought maybe that night I would join my father again, but that did not happen.

That day, my second inside Auschwitz, was the last time I ever saw my father.

The Germans dragged me to the laundry. Whether they wanted me first to perform a simpler task than mechanical work, or whether this was a punishment for trying to flee, I do not know. But after my sprinting stunt, I was eager to show the Germans I was a hard worker who could be of use.

My first job in the camps was washing Nazi uniforms. I knew nothing of the task. In Pavlovo we had a maid who washed all my clothes. Still, I grabbed a brush and an SS soldier's shirt and scrubbed hard and fast. After working my way about halfway through the pile, it happened. I scrubbed so hard the bristles ripped the collar. The face of the pacing soldier at my station flushed red. I do not remember his words, but I remember his baton. He beat me until I bled. He needed to make an example out of me for the other prisoners. When he was finished with my flogging, he balled up the torn shirt and threw it in my face before huffing off.

The shirt was trash to the soldier but not to me. I kept it. Working in the laundry was a nice man who knew how to sew. He gave me a needle and thread and taught me how to sew a simple stitch.

I mended the shirt. To this day I still don't know why, but when I got up the courage, I slipped the soldier's shirt on and wore it under my striped prisoner uniform. It was a crazy thing to do, because none of the other prisoners had a shirt. But I did it anyhow. From that day on, the soldiers treated me a little bit better. They thought I was somebody—someone who mattered, someone not to be killed. The prisoners treated me a little bit better as well. You must remember that some of the *kapos* (supervisors) were Jewish prisoners, but they could be brutal. They wanted to please the Germans, so some of them would be hard on us so the Germans would not punish them. Sometimes the *kapos* were harsher than some of the Germans. When I had my soldier shirt on, however, that did not happen. When I wore the shirt, the *kapos* didn't mess with me.

The shirt means something, I thought. And so, I wore the shirt. In fact, I ripped another one on purpose so I could have two.

The day I first wore that shirt was the day I learned clothes possess power. Clothes don't just "make the man," they can save the man. They did for me.

Of course, receiving your first tailoring lesson inside a Nazi concentration camp was hardly the ideal apprenticeship. I would have much preferred to hone my craft on Savile Row or in the mills of Milan. Looking back, though, that moment in the camps marked the beginning of the rest of my life. Strangely enough, two ripped Nazi shirts helped this *Jew* build America's most famous and successful custom-suit company.

God has a wonderful sense of humor.

CHAPTER TWO

INSIDE AUSCHWITZ

Many days inside Auschwitz I was afraid I would die—and then afraid I wouldn't.

We were surrounded by death and darkness, madness and murder. And the vicious precision and regimented order of the place made the moral insanity all the more bizarre and cruel.

Each morning around 4:30 we were stirred from our sleep, lined up, and counted in a ritual known as roll call. My heart would start jumping in my chest. A Nazi soldier would whirl his baton and scan the line with his eyes while another called out the list of prisoner numbers. Any sign of illness or fatigue was cause for being pulled from the line and sent to the crematorium.

Day and night the ovens burned. The smoke spewed up from the soaring brick chimney and belched the vaporous remnants of corpses into the air. At night you could see the flames spitting against the blackened sky. Still, no one in the camps talked to me about the crematoria. Whether that was because I was just a boy or because I no longer had a father by my side to speak piercing truths to me, I do not know. But I could smell that something was horribly wrong.

After morning roll call, we were given something approximating black coffee. To be sick or weak was dangerous, so no matter how rancid the gruel or vile the smell, I forced myself to eat. The afternoon slop was usually some sort of soup that frequently had human hair, trash, or dead insects floating in it. Sundown brought black bread mixed with sawdust. Soup made you skinny. Bread made strength. So I ate as much bread as I could scavenge and always tried to cover my wounds with my clothes.

My labor assignment in the laundry lasted several days before I was moved to the sorting room, which housed the confiscated wares of newly arrived prisoners. The space was filled with fifty or so prisoners combing and sifting mountains of clothes, shoes, and other possessions. Sometimes a prisoner stumbled upon a hidden morsel of food folded inside a bag or tucked inside a coat pocket. Prisoners caught trying to sneak a bite were promptly whipped by a *kapo*, who often smuggled the food or ate it himself.

Between the rummaging and sorting, I peeked over and around piles every chance I got in the hopes of spotting a family member. That's all I wanted: one glimpse, a single fleeting confirmation they were still alive. But it never came. Looking back now I realize that false, cruel wish, like an invisible ladder whose rungs materialized based on hope, compelled me to reach for survival.

The weeks passed and the piles got smaller and smaller until transports of new prisoners slowed to a trickle. The Nazis reassigned me to the bricklaying teams. Allied bombs were busting up brick buildings everywhere, so our services were in high demand. I knew nothing about masonry. A prisoner who served as a team leader stuck a trowel in my one hand and a mortar bucket in the other before walking me to a block of bricks. There I learned the finer points of bricklaying before being put to work.

The work was hard and the days were long, and my wire-thin teenage frame did its best to keep up with the older, stronger men. For some reason, slathering and smoothing the mortar across the faces of the bricks made my thoughts float to Pavlovo and brought back scenes of Grandma Geitel icing freshly baked cakes. Before long I had perfected my ability to detach my mind from my physical form, and my body sped up as my thoughts slowed down.

Even so, no matter how hard we worked, our captors would slay prisoners without provocation.

Killings were frequent and random. One day a boy from my block and I were tasked with building a brick wall. We started just after morning lineup. By late afternoon we had completed a good stretch of the wall and felt a certain pride in our accomplishment. We stacked the bricks higher and higher until the wall stood some five or six feet tall. We talked while working to unclench our minds. A single gunshot rang out, but I didn't think much of it. The crack of rifle fire and the spraying of machine guns were common, so I kept stacking and talking. I asked the boy a question and got no reply.

I asked again.

Silence.

I swiveled my head in his direction. Several yards away, the boy lay motionless, facedown in the dirt inside an expanding pool of blood. I later learned a Nazi had used the boy for target practice.

At home in Pavlovo—and in most civilizations—a clear moral order structured our daily lives. Hard work, justice, fairness, integrity—these virtues produced predictable fruits. But not in the concentration camps. The Germans killed for any reason or none at all. It was futile to try to discern their logic, because there was none. If a Nazi was angry, he might kill you. If a Nazi was happy, he might kill you. It made no difference.

The dehumanizing randomness of the murders suffocated my sense of hope, just as Hitler and his henchmen had intended. What appeared random was, in fact, not random at all. It was a systematic psychological lynching, a strangling of the human heart's need to believe in the rewards of goodness, a snapping of the moral hinge on which humanity swings. Soon, and much to my shame, I became anesthetized to death, numb to depravity. Some primal survival switch inside me had been temporarily flicked on that allowed me to submerge the emotions generated by the evil scorching my eyes.

I witnessed dozens of shootings and helped carry scores of corpses. Sometimes a dead body would be intact and appear to be sleeping. Other times a bullet would rip through a prisoner, spilling out organs. Or shatter a skull, exposing chunks of brain. But as the days passed, no matter its condition, a body soon became just a body, a sallow, bloodless, gangling object that must be lugged, heaved atop a pile, or dropped in a hole. At fifteen, I had become an undertaker.

But children even younger than I were plunged into the same abyss. What's more, I had already learned to survive on my own during my years living in Budapest at the brothel and working as a mechanic. Sometimes I think God used those years as a sort of training ground, a kind of boot camp, to prepare me for my orphaned existence.

Some days inside Auschwitz seemed to evaporate one into another, mornings ebbing into evenings with mind-numbing monotony. Other days brought jarring events that, decades later, still visit me in vivid nightmares. Like the first time another prisoner beat me.

During morning roll call, an SS soldier barked my number. *This is it,* I thought. *You're about to become one of the disappeared.* The soldier pulled me from the line and ordered me off to the side, away from the others. I stood there for over an hour. Sometimes the lineup took hours, as the Germans counted over and over and over to make sure every last miserable one of us was accounted for. It mattered little whether we were alive or had died the night before in the sleeping racks. Every skeleton must be catalogued and counted.

The Nazis then yanked another boy off the line and ordered him to stand alongside me. The boy and I had never spoken. From the looks of him, he appeared to be a few years older; he was at least six inches taller.

The rest of the prisoners were dispersed to begin their daily slave labor. The boy and I were marched to a room inside a building

I had never been in before. When we entered, the walls echoed with the cracks of whips and the cries of men.

Scattered throughout the space were small clusters of prisoners, each with one or two SS soldiers interrogating them. The Nazi walked my fellow inmate and me to a clear patch in the room and poked his baton into my sternum.

"Is your father a partisan?" he asked.

"No, my father is not a partisan," I said.

"I'll ask again. Is your father a partisan?" he said louder.

"No. No, he is not," I replied.

"Where is your father now?" said the soldier.

"I don't know," I said. "Somewhere in the concentration camps."

"Tell me his number."

"I do not know his number."

"Tell me his number right now!"

"I do not know it," I said, lying in the hope of protecting my father.

"Down! On the ground!" he barked.

I crouched down on all fours. The soldier turned to my fellow inmate.

"You! Whip him hard! Now!" the soldier commanded.

I looked back over my shoulder and saw the German hand the boy what appeared to be a stick. "Whip him! Now!" ordered the German. The boy knew what we all knew: any attempt to be merciful and strike with anything less than full force would mean instant punishment. I stared straight ahead, my muscles tightening in anticipation of the first lash. The boy cocked back his arm and let the whip crack right between my shoulder blades. My elbows buckled. The sting undulated across my back.

"Again!" yelled the soldier. The second lash tore across the small of my back. I screamed. "Another!" yelled the Nazi. My arms quavered as my body grew heavier. The third strike of the stick hit square against my spine, sending me falling face-first to the floor. Tears streaked my dirty face. The soldier ordered me to stand.

"Is your father a partisan?" the soldier asked again, this time with a smile.

"I cannot lie. My father is *not* a partisan. He is *not*," I said.

"We'll see about that," he said. The soldier turned and glared at the other boy.

"What about your father? A partisan?" asked the soldier.

"No. He is not," answered the boy. The soldier stabbed the air with his baton in a downward motion. "Down!"

The boy assumed the position. The German handed me the whipping stick I'd just been beaten with. "Whip him! Hard!" the Nazi commanded. I looked down at the bludgeon and saw that it was smeared pink with my blood.

"Whip him!"

I reared back my arm and drove the whip into the middle of the boy's back.

"Another!"

It was at this moment that I realized the boy had intentionally spaced out my lashes as a favor to me. I tried to return the compassion, this time aiming lower. The boy howled and his knees gave

way. I'd missed and struck his tailbone. Everything in me wanted
to apologize to him for the misplaced hit. But I knew any hint of
tenderness or decency would be met with swift SS intervention
against us both.

"Again!"

This time I focused hard on the top of his back and aimed
squarely for his shoulder blades, the largest unstruck portion of his
back. The stick landed right on target.

"Up! Up! Up!"

The boy sprung off the ground and stood at attention.

"Is your father a partisan?" the soldier asked him.

"No, he is not a partisan. I do not know where he is. But he is
not a partisan at all."

My eyes darted across the room. The same sordid scene, prisoner flogging prisoner, was unfolding all around us, as Nazis
played conductor in their sadistic symphony.

*What had my people done to deserve this? How could they
hate us this much when they didn't even know our names?* There
were no answers to my youthfully naïve questions.

"Back to your block!" snapped the soldier.

The rest of the day, my mind whirred. *Was Father being tor-
tured? Did he say something that tipped them off? Did Father give
them my prisoner number?* The psychological torment was almost
as painful as the welts stinging my back.

The next morning's roll call played out like the last. The same
boy and I were ordered off the line, hauled to the interrogation
room, and forced to trade blows while attempting to shield our
fathers from danger. With each denial we gave—"No, my father
is not a partisan"—I felt a strange pang of pride, a small celebration

of victory that neither of us had sold out his own blood, even as we were forced to spill each other's.

Five days straight. That's how long they made us beat each other. Not once did either of us give up his father.

I'd endured nearly a week of beatings. My back was criss-crossed with deep trenches of torn skin. I couldn't see the wounds, but I could feel the blood pool inside the ripped grooves before spilling over and oozing down my back. I tried to make a game of standing and sitting in such a way so as to keep my shirt from brushing against my lacerated skin.

The day after my final beating, I walked into my barrack, only to be accosted by a German I had never seen before. He was a doctor, the kind whose job it was to play God in a medical ritual known as *Muselmann* inspection. *Muselmann* was the word we used in the camps to describe a walking, emaciated corpse. Doctors determined whether a sick or malnourished prisoner was salvageable or whether he should be gassed and burned. My heart jumped when I saw the *Muselmann* doctor.

The doctor spun me around, lifted my striped uniform and Nazi shirt, and fingered the loose meaty flap of flesh barely covering exposed muscle. "Tomorrow there is a transport going to Buna," he said flatly. "Your number is on it. You will be on the transport." He asked no questions and offered no explanations. But for whatever reason, that German doctor decided to save my life. I never saw him again.

Five miles from Auschwitz in Poland lay the subcamp of Monowitz, or "Buna." The name Buna was derived from the

butadiene synthetic rubber factory there that was owned by the IG
Farben chemical conglomerate. The SS sold prisoners to IG Farben
to work as slave laborers in their massive industrial factories where,
among other things, the company manufactured the Zyklon B gas
used to exterminate my people.

From factory work to excavation to bricklaying to bookkeep-
ing, IG Farben demanded slave laborers with all manner of trades
and skills. The work conditions were as grueling as at Auschwitz,
complete with eleven-hour workdays most of the year and thirteen-
hour shifts in the summer. But since IG Farben paid for the prisoners, the Nazis were less inclined to kill off inmates for fun. Instead,
soldiers administered punishments by singling prisoners out for
life-threatening labor assignments such as working in the mines.
Nevertheless, in the little over two years of the Buna concentration
camp's existence, the Germans sent an estimated twenty-three
thousand prisoners to their deaths.

When I arrived in Buna, I said nothing and complained to no
one about my back. Buna had a hospital, but I reasoned that asking
for medical assistance might be a one-way ticket to death. Suffering
in silence was foolish; infection felled prisoners regularly. But the
alternative—seeking medical attention—was a far swifter death
sentence than the most virulent disease.

If I die I die, I thought.

The Buna barracks were overcrowded and shoddily constructed. During my first week there, I woke up drenched in sweat
and trembling with the chills. With no way to hide my condition,
I gambled and quietly asked a *kapo* for help. He said he would try
to get me into the hospital to see a doctor without raising any
alarms about my condition to the soldiers.

The doctor I saw was himself a prisoner. To my amazement, he said he knew my dad. The connection to my father—no matter how tenuous—lifted my spirits.

"Your assignments are reinjuring your back," the doctor explained. "The weight, the bending, the lifting—your wounds can't heal properly. They'll never heal, so long as you're doing hard manual labor." He said he would have me reassigned to work inside the hospital. I was overjoyed.

Even though I'll be around sick and dying people, I thought, *at least there will be no more slayings inside the hospital.*

I was wrong. Instead of gunshots, the Nazis in the hospital administered death sentences with a lethal dose of phenol injected into the heart.

Doctors often conducted morning roll call for hospital patients. There was a silent code of support among some of the prisoner doctors and inmates. When a doctor saw a prisoner with a dire condition or in distress, he would try to get the patient better medicines or extra food rations. I joined the discreet team effort in any little way I could. When a feeble patient was in danger of being singled out, I volunteered to stand in for him.

The doctors weren't stupid; they knew what I was doing. Tragically, a lot of the sick ended up dying anyway because they were so weak. Only a few of the truly sick patients got well and returned to work in the camps. Still, even though my efforts weren't much—I was just a kid—patients' eyes glowed with gratitude every time I told them I would take their place in line. I guess it made them feel worth something and restored a sliver of their human dignity. It did the same for me, too.

One of my jobs in the Buna hospital was preparing and delivering rations of "soup." With my Nazi shirt under my uniform, no one questioned my coming and going. Operating somewhat invisibly allowed me to get more food to more people. On one occasion I brought a person from my town extra portions several days in a row until he finally regained his strength. God helped him survive, not me. But it made my heart happy to have God use me in a small way to bring someone I knew back to health.

Working in the hospital, I saw every type of malady imaginable. Bloated bodies, corpses covered with disfiguring rashes, skeletons with skin stretched tight like a drum, bodies with limbs blown apart by bombs—I saw it all and helped haul carcasses out of the hospital.

Buna's barrack conditions were no less bestial than those in Auschwitz. We were so tightly packed into our sleeping racks that everyone had to learn to turn or readjust in unison. Despite the Germans' desire to prevent outbreaks of typhus or malaria, hygiene was horrific. One shower a week was a luxury. It was not uncommon while sleeping to be urinated or defecated on by fellow prisoners. Nighttime thefts were also a problem. Sometimes a prisoner might save and hide a scrap of black bread, only to have another prisoner pilfer and eat it.

After my back healed, I was taken off hospital detail and reassigned to work in the Buna Works factory and to do brick repairs on bombed-out buildings. Once, while working in the factory, I was assigned to feed wooden planks into a cutting machine. I got distracted and took my eyes off the boards. The machine severed one of my fingers and nearly took off my hand.

The industrial importance of Buna's rubber factory made it an Allied bombing target. I recall at least twice being bombed at Buna. The first time was December 18, 1944. The warning sirens blared as the rumble of American B-17 and B-24 bomber planes thundered overhead. I scrambled to hide under something and prayed the bombs would miss us and kill our captors.

The shockwave and blast of bombs excited me. With every bomb the Americans dropped, I knew we were that much closer to liberation. Instead of manna, God dropped munitions. The aftermath was glorious. Fires raged, and black columns of smoke rose not from crematoria chimneys but from the rubble of the German factory.

The Americans pounded Buna with another massive payload eight days later. This time when the sirens sounded, I noticed something I had missed during the last bombing raid: the sight of the SS scurrying and hiding like cockroaches exposed to the light. *How beautiful to see them fear for their own lives for once,* I thought. *How wonderful that they must finally confront a force superior to their own.*

When the all clear sounded, the soldiers crawled out from their crevices and resumed their stations. But for that brief moment when the bombs rained down on Buna, they, too, were reminded of their own mortality, submissive to the might of the bombs, made to cower in fear. Seeing that felt good. Damn good.

CHAPTER THREE

THE DEATH MARCH

1945. Winter battered Buna.

Having grown up in the Carpathian Mountains, I thought I was adjusted to blistering winds and icy nights. I wasn't. At night my hands and feet went numb clutching the thin blanket the Germans gave us. It was not uncommon to wake up to find prisoners frozen to death in the sleeping racks.

The bombing raids before the new year raised our spirits. But rumors of Russian and American forces tightening the noose on Hitler were common. Prior bombings had failed to bring liberation, but this time seemed different. This time, I'd felt the ground shake beneath my feet.

The blocks buzzed with chatter about a possible evacuation. By the middle of January the Russian cannons closed in on the camp. With over ten thousand prisoners still in Buna, where we would go or how we would get there no one knew. My hand injury had put me back working in the hospital. One thing I knew for certain was that the hundreds of infirmed prisoners could barely move, let alone survive relocation.

A few days later, our block leader assembled us to confirm the rumors: we would evacuate the next night. The Germans' plan was to empty dozens of subcamps and march tens of thousands of prisoners to the central meeting point of Gleiwitz. The walking wake became known as the Death March.

What one wore could determine whether one lived. Prisoners scrambled to gather extra garments and to double-wrap wounds. Others stuffed straw from sleeping-rack mattresses or empty cement sacks into their uniform to insulate themselves against the brutal cold. I raced to the hospital and grabbed a coveted pair of socks, a shirt, and a jacket. Foot care was a major ordeal in the concentration camps. Prisoners were not issued socks. The only "shoes" we had were wooden, Dutch-style clogs with weak linen straps. After hours of walking or running, feet blistered and skin sloughed off on the wooden soles. I'd seen enough pus-filled foot infections and frostbite cases in the hospital to know foot care would be essential for surviving the roughly twenty-five snow-covered miles between Buna and Gleiwitz.

The Germans gave us extra bread and thin blankets. At sundown the SS organized the blocks into thousand-man columns. Fathers huddled with sons in the hopes of being put in the same group to Gleiwitz. How I yearned to be one of those father-son pairs.

I fell in with the hospital unit. Only the well and walking were allowed to make the march. We left roughly 850 ill prisoners behind in Buna. When the Russians arrived days later to liberate Buna, 250 of those prisoners had already died; others were too far gone to ever recover.

A doctor in our column ordered me to help push the medicine supply wagon. I tried to stay positive.

Maybe being close to life-saving medicines and having a cart to lean on will help steady my stride, I told myself.

A stillness fell over the column. Searchlights lit up the camp. I looked straight ahead toward the gate. Puffs of breath hovered in the icy air above rows of cap-covered heads standing and waiting in our column. I shook my arms and pumped my legs to keep my blood flowing in the bitter cold while we waited.

"Forward! March!"

I leaned hard into the wagon to turn the wheels just a few inches, lowering my head as we passed through the gate to let the bracing wind roll over my back. "Faster!" the SS yelled. I steadied my breathing and emptied my mind, just as I'd learned to do during so many bricklaying missions.

Gear inside the wagon clattered and clanked as I sloshed through the snow. I angled my body into the rolling pharmacy to shift my weight off my feet and onto the wagon. The wind whipped our faces as the snow fell hard against the blackness. The march would be the ultimate endurance test, one in which the mind must master the body. I paid no attention to the rumblings from my stomach and imagined warmth instead.

"Faster! Faster! Faster!"

The wagon rattled as I ran. Wheezing prisoners sucked cold air deep into their lungs. Huffing, hissing, tubercular coughing filled the night sky as we crunched through the unrelenting snow.

Slowing down or resting brought instant death. Anyone who faltered or fell was executed on the spot. The first couple miles brought intermittent pistol pops, but the farther we marched the more gunshots I heard. I had long since stopped flinching at the sound of gunfire. Slayings had become a common feature of our cursed existence. Our column had become a moving shooting gallery.

The medicine wagon's wheels, slick with sludge, became easier to roll. Still, the cart's weight and resistance wore on my arms, back, and atrophied leg muscles. The farther we went, the thicker the snow mounds grew until the wheels of the wagon stopped turning. Why we'd taken the medicine wagon in the first place was a mystery to me. The Nazis would have never permitted prisoners to use the rolling pharmacy; our health was hardly their concern. What's more, most of the soldiers' packs were loaded with vital emergency medicine kits and food rations, rendering the wagon's contents useless to the SS as well.

Blasts of wind sent the snow slamming diagonally across our column, and I knew I would never make it to Gleiwitz pushing the medicine wagon. We pressed on. A doctor saw me grinding like a mule against the cart. "The wagon is of no use. Leave it," he said. I lifted my hands off the cart and quickly stepped around it to avoid breaking stride or catching a soldier's eye. My body lunged forward without the wagon's weight, sending me bumping into the prisoner in front of me. "Watch it!" snapped the prisoner. The rest of the column veered around the sides of the cart like fish swimming around a rock.

About an hour after I ditched the wagon, I noticed that some German soldiers had begun ordering prisoners to haul their heavy rucksacks. A few minutes later a German trotted up alongside me. "Put this on and carry it," he said without breaking stride. He slipped the pack on my shoulders. Its weight—at least thirty pounds, a significant burden given my small frame and condition—threw me off balance and nearly toppled me to the ground.

What is this bastard lugging? A dead body?

The twisted thought made me chuckle under my breath.

Gunshots now rang with regularity. My hunger was too intense to ignore. I slipped a piece of black bread from inside my jacket and ate it. I ran with my mouth agape in the hopes of catching a few snowflakes to wet my tongue.

While I was chewing the bread and licking the icy air, a gust of wind smacked the side of our column and temporarily bent our formation. The sting of the wind and force of the blast jolted me out of my tunnel vision, reminding me that there was a world surrounding the hallway of horror down which we clomped. I looked to my sides at the ghastly scenes on our flanks as bullet-riddled bodies lay strewn across the snow.

We trudged on. The soldier's pack on my back was about to cause a crisis. I had to do something. Fast. The soldier it belonged to was nowhere in sight. I peered over my shoulder and spotted two boys I knew from the camp. I caught their eyes and motioned for them to catch up to me. "What is it?" the boy to my right asked softly.

"You hungry?" I asked.

"Yes," he said.

"Starving!" said the other boy in a hushed voice.

"I think I can help," I said. "I think this bag has food rations."

"Are you crazy?!" the voice over my right shoulder said.

"He'll kill you if he finds food missing!" said the other.

"Yeah, but at least I won't die hungry!" I joked.

They were not amused.

"Fine," I said. "Just unbuckle the sack and tell me what's inside."

"What if they see us?" the boy on the left said.

"They won't. Besides, like you said, he'll shoot me. Not you."

Several paces later I felt a gentle tug against my back as one of the boys loosed the strap and unlatched the closure. Under the cover of darkness, he lifted the flap and rummaged through the bag with his hand. "There's bread in there, wurst, a heavy metal ammunition box, and a medicine pack," he said.

"No human head?" I quipped. My exhaustion was making me silly. "Grab the heavy box and toss it," I said.

"You've gone mad," one of them said.

"Fine, I'll throw it away," I said. "Just hand me the box low on my right."

The boy on my right pressed the box against my hip and passed it to me. I marched ten paces or so before dropping the heavy object into a deep snowdrift and watching it disappear. My load felt much lighter.

The blasts of the Russian cannon pounding the German lines, like a military cadence, kept me motivated and moving. But the hunger—that damn hunger—wouldn't relent. My feet were now frozen blocks. It felt as if I were jogging on stilts.

I needed energy. "Hand me the bread," I said over my shoulder. "I will share." The boy on my right wasted no time. His hand stabbed into the bag like a spear, poached the loaf, and handed it to me.

"Here," I said, "share this." I ripped off a chunk and passed the bread like a relay baton behind me. Both boys' hands clawed for the German's bread—far fresher than our own fare. I slipped a piece of the soft loaf into my mouth and closed my eyes briefly to savor it. It was the best bread I ever tasted—even better than my mother's and grandmother's homemade loaves. I swirled my tongue over and around the fluffy morsel to soak up the taste.

I paused for a moment before requesting the wurst. My family kept kosher, but given the circumstances, I figured God would understand. "Hand me the wurst," I said. I bit off a mouthful of salty meat. It tasted funny. I gnawed off two more pieces and handed them to the boys.

Our evening meal and reverie were short-lived. The front of our column was marching into walls of wind and snow. "March! March! March!" the SS officer barked. Bodies dropped fast in the worsening weather and were left behind. To quench their punishing thirst, prisoners ate the snow that piled up on themselves and the men marching in front of them.

"I have to rest," I heard an unfamiliar voice say behind me. "Just a minute. It's not in me to keep...." The man fell forward, and I felt his fingertips brush my backpack, as if he was trying to break his fall. I kept marching. A few paces later I looked over my shoulder and saw a flash from an SS gun and the man's body twitching in the snow.

Prisoners tumbled and were trampled in a crescendo of gun blasts. We passed corpse after corpse as drifts of snow covered the dead. We kept going. The more bodies I saw, the more paranoid I became that the soldier would reclaim his pilfered pack and shoot me in the head. The burn in my thighs and the sting of the cold in my eyes made me lightheaded.

If he shoots you, he shoots you, I thought. *There's nothing you can do about it. Might as well take the medicines too.*

Where this idea came from I have no idea. It was risky. Despite working in the hospital and pushing the medicine wagon, I had no training in pharmacology. The pills could have been vitamins or poison. I wouldn't have known the difference. Either way, the pills couldn't worsen my condition. If they killed me, I was out of my misery. If they boosted my system, I had a better chance of survival. I decided I'd swallow them if and when we ever stopped.

We'd marched for miles without ceasing. I'd pissed myself twice, the urine warming my legs as it trickled down. The SS must have been getting tired as well because a German finally ordered us to halt. Prisoners collapsed as if their spines had been yanked out by a string.

I stretched out my arms and let my body fall backward like a spruce into a pillow of snow. My head spun as I stared up at the sky. Stars winked against the blackness. I'd never felt so alone. I wondered where God was, where He'd been these last nine months. Many of the older religious men in the camps had remained faithful, had prayed nightly. I admired their deep faith, their commitment to never letting go of God. I wasn't having a crisis of faith. I

was a child. I didn't think grand, deep thoughts. All I knew was
that I wanted to feel close to God, to know He hadn't forgotten
me and still loved me.

Maybe God's just been really busy, I remember thinking. *Soon
maybe He will remember me.*

I turned my head away from the sky and looked out across the
frozen wasteland. Men lay heaving and writhing from cramps or
illnesses unknown. I didn't know the time but figured it must be
hours still before dawn. I knew that long before any of us had a
chance to replenish his broken body with rest, the SS would have
us up and marching again. I wanted to sleep. The snow blanketing
the ground reminded me of Pavlovo in winter, reminded me of
Grandfather Abraham and his strong horses galloping through the
snows. I sat up with legs bent to keep my pants dry and hugged
my knees and rocked back and forth, lost in thought for nearly an
hour until I felt a tap on my shoulder.

"What are you going to do now?" a voice asked. I turned
around. It was the boy on my right who'd marched behind me and
retrieved items from the soldier's pack.

"What?" I said confused.

"What are you going to do when light comes and he finds
you?"

"Who?"

"The soldier! The one who owns the bag," he said pointing to
the sack. I'd forgotten I even had it.

"The medicine kit!" I said. "I forgot to take the pills!" I
unlatched the bag and tore open the kit and popped the pills into
my mouth, forcing them down my throat with a handful of snow.

"What in the hell did you just take?" the boy asked.

"Don't know. Don't worry about it."

"Soon he'll find you. What then? What will you say?"

He was right. With the column thinned out from deaths, and sunlight just hours away, chances were I'd be caught and killed. My heart jumped.

"I need you to bury me," I said.

"You're not dead yet!"

"No, I mean bury me while I'm still alive. Underneath the snow, before they start moving again. That way he won't find me."

"You'll freeze and then you'll really be dead."

"We'll wait as long as we can. I'll pick out a place and get it ready while everyone rests. Then, when the time is right, you will hide me under the snow."

He promised to help and said he'd get the other boy to assist as well. I got up and stepped around resting prisoners to find the perfect spot, one that blended in so as not to arouse suspicion. The best plot for my snow burial was an embankment several paces back up the path we'd come down. The dip in the embankment would make digging out easier. The key would be smoothing the snow to cover the portal where I'd entered so that it looked natural and untouched.

I tunneled into the slope, piling the snow next to the hole so the boys could cover me quickly. I rejoined the group and found the boys. "Be sure to smooth the snow after you bury me," I urged. "Make sure to cover your footprints so they don't see any tracks."

"It's snowing so hard it won't matter," said one of the boys. "But yes, we'll smooth it."

About an hour later, men started stirring about and gathering their gear. I wanted to give the boys enough time to smooth the snow properly. "This way. Let's go!" I said. When we got to the spot, the hole had already refilled with snow. I dug it out and hopped in. "Remember to smooth it out and cover your tracks," I pleaded. They nodded in unison and waited for me to crawl in. I pulled my jacket up over my head. "Okay. Cover me up," I said. The boys had fun taking turns dumping piles of powder on my head. I sat crouched in a vertical fetal position and created a space between my knees to breathe.

"We're smoothing it now," a muffled voice said from above. I sat still inside my crystalline cocoon. "We're going back now. Good luck!"

The makeshift womb that shielded me from the whipping winds wasn't nearly as cold as I'd anticipated. I sat and listened intently. About a half hour later, I heard a faint noise that sounded like a call to march. But I wasn't sure. I waited a little longer before slowly cracking the surface with a single finger, like a baby chick breaking its shell. I waited and listened but heard nothing.

I pushed my body up slowly until my eyes could survey the quiet and colorless world outside. I burst through the snow pile and crawled on all fours down the embankment. I looked up the road. No one. I looked down the road. Nothing. "It worked," I muttered softly. "It worked!"

I dusted the snow off my clothes and wrung the wetness out of my shirt bottoms and socks before tromping up the track to where we had gathered hours before. The sight before me made me stop. Scores of frozen frames lay littered across the land, embalmed in glacial graves. The wind whistled past me as I stood and stared at the stiff, bloodless bodies. They looked so peaceful, like souls who had chosen to remain in their dreams rather than reawaken in this nightmare. A part of me envied their peace.

I walked past the unburied and back down to the road. I was all alone. At that moment I could have escaped and run away. But to where and for what? I was an orphan and a target. I decided it was best to take my chances getting to Gleiwitz. *The soldier probably thinks I died or got shot,* I thought. My mind was made up: I would return to captivity.

As it turned out, we were only a mile or two from Gleiwitz when we'd stopped. With waves of subcamps converging on Gleiwitz, the SS were exhausted from the marches and rattled by the Russians' unrelenting onslaught—so much so that we were allowed to feast on the remnants of a hastily abandoned dinner in the Germans' barracks. I helped dole out portions to the frozen, skeletal prisoners staggering into the camp. Months later a prisoner told me I saved his life by giving him double.

I ate better at Gleiwitz than at any other time throughout my Shoah experience. I stuffed as much food in my clothes as possible. In time, I felt surprisingly healthy. I told myself that the soldier's medicines must have been vitamins that boosted my system. Whether that was true or not, the pills at least acted as a placebo that strengthened my mind and emboldened me to carry on.

After a night or two at Gleiwitz, the Nazis herded us to the train depot and packed us into roofless coal cars. We clacked along the tracks for four impossible days. The speed of the train made the wind chill colder than the Death March. Many people froze to death in the cars. The Nazis had long since pushed us past concern for ceremony. The minute a person expired, we chucked the corpse out of the car to free up space so we could crouch lower to dodge the brutal winds. I reminded myself to shift my legs and flex what was left of my muscles to keep the blood moving.

I stared down the row of coal cars at the jostling cap-covered heads and pondered what a cursed lot we were. The faces inside my car were remote and waxen, their eyes vacant and fixed on nothing. Every few miles a car in front would hurl someone's dead father or son to the tracks. Stoic German faces stared at us as we rode through small towns.

When space allowed, we lit a small fire in the car. Prisoners clambered toward the flames to thaw themselves as the Germans hauled us to yet another destination unknown.

CHAPTER FOUR

IKE ARRIVES

Buchenwald concentration camp. Our train stopped on February 5, 1945, at a railway station in central Germany, five miles north of Weimar.

We ascended the hill leading up to our new hell. Incorporated into the iron gate was the slogan *Jedem das Seine* ("To each what he deserves"). Another sign on the gatehouse wall read *Recht oder Unrecht mein Vaterland* ("My country, right or wrong").

The camp's grand scale and exacting design were a testament to the Nazis' dedication to Hitler's "Final Solution." Buchenwald was one of Germany's biggest concentration camps, holding eighty-nine thousand prisoners at its peak. When I arrived, there were half that many inmates. Of the 240,000 prisoners who entered Buchenwald's gates, at least 55,000 perished.

I schlepped forward in the processing line. All around me were bedraggled prisoners. The macabre routine had become all too familiar: strip naked, race to a bathhouse, sit while clippers rip out chunks of your hair, brace for the excruciating sting of disinfectant, don ridiculous prisoner pajamas and clownish wooden clogs, endure all manner of verbal degradation and physical brutality, receive your slave labor assignment, get a barracks number.

Whatever fear was in me evaporated. I had come face-to-face with the Angel of Death at Auschwitz and seen my family torn away from me. I had survived the bombing raids at Buna, narrowly made it through the frozen Death March to Gleiwitz, and endured the brutal four-day train ride to Buchenwald in an open coal car. The Nazis' ignorance and savagery enraged me. Enough was enough. All I wanted was all I'd ever known. I wanted my family and my freedom.

I got Block 58 instead.

Inside, Buchenwald was a typical Nazi death mill, complete with crematoria, execution rooms, and a hospital the Germans used for medical experimentation. The camp had one notable exception: it lacked gas chambers. The Germans fully intended to install them, but brave prisoners in the underground resistance groups stymied their plans by intercepting and destroying telegraphed directives. Without the prisoners' courage, I and tens of thousands more would likely have been annihilated.

My forty-five thousand fellow inmates came from thirty countries, and they included American, English, Canadian, and Russian prisoners of war. Hitler's "undesirables" were there, too—Jehovah's Witnesses, Gypsies, homosexuals, the physically and mentally disabled, and others.

Block 58 sat in Buchenwald's infamous "Little Camp," a shoddily built quarantine overflow facility surrounded by barbed wire. Eating and sleeping conditions were deplorable. The only improvement: 44,999 new pallid faces among which to search for my father.

Roll calls at Buchenwald were more frequent and meticulous than I'd experienced at the other camps. When the order to assemble blared through the loudspeaker, we swarmed out of our barracks like ants onto the massive *Appelplatz* near the main gate. Reeling from the Allies' surge, the Nazis counted on slave labor more than ever, and their obsession with counting and recounting prisoners intensified. Even so, whippings were regular, and deaths from malnutrition and disease were constant. Buchenwald soldiers fixated on prisoners making their "beds" properly. Seeing inmates savagely whipped for creased blankets, I made sure my ratty blanket lay flat and smooth across my rack.

The SS assigned me to work in the munitions factory. But early one morning after roll call, a soldier placed me on a twelve-prisoner team to perform repairs outside the camp in nearby Weimar. Working in the city was a welcome distraction from camp life. Sometimes you got lucky and spotted a potato in a field or smuggled a trinket to trade for food. Either way, it was a chance to see the sky, escape the stench of rotting corpses, and confirm that there was still a world beyond the barbed wire.

We loaded our gear and marched the few miles to Weimar. The soldiers stopped us in front of a bombed-out mansion, home to the mayor of Weimar. A big black Mercedes sat out front. The soldiers commanded us to sift the rubble, clear the debris, and begin repairs on the mansion.

I walked alone to the back of the estate to assess the damage. Dusty piles of broken bricks lay scattered across the yard. Seeing the cellar door ajar, I slowly opened it. A shaft of sunlight filled the dank cellar. On one side of the space sat a wooden cage wrapped in chicken wire. I walked closer and noticed two quivering rabbits inside the cage. "They're still alive!" I said to myself with surprise. Inside the cage were the remains of the rabbits' dinner.

I unlatched the cage and pulled out a wilted leaf and carrot nub. The lettuce was browning and slimy, the carrot still moist from the rabbits' gnawing. Excited, I wolfed down the lettuce and tried to crack the chunk of carrot in half with my teeth.

My luck was short-lived. "What are you doing?" a voice yelled.

I whipped my head around toward the door. A gorgeous, smartly dressed blond woman holding a baby stood silhouetted in the doorframe. It was the mayor of Weimar's wife.

"I...I found your rabbits!" I stammered with a cheerful nervousness. "They're alive and safe!"

"Why in the *hell* are you stealing my rabbits' food?" barked the woman. "Animal!" I stood silent and stared at the floor.

"I'm reporting this immediately!" she said, stomping away. My heart pounded in my emaciated chest. A few minutes later, an SS soldier ordered me to come out of the cellar. I knew what was coming, and the knowing made it all the worse.

"Down on the ground, you dog! Fast!" yelled the German. He gripped his baton and bludgeoned my back. I do not know whether the mayor's wife watched the beating. Given her cruelty, why would she want to miss it? On the hike back to Buchenwald, I replayed the scene over and over in my mind.

How could a woman carrying her own child find a walking skeleton saving her pets and have him beaten for nibbling on rotten animal food? I thought.

In that moment my numbness to death melted. In its place rose an alien bloodlust, a hunger for vengeance unlike any I had ever known. The surge of adrenaline and rush of rage felt good inside my withered frame. Then and there I made a vow to myself: if I survived Buchenwald, I would return and kill the mayor's wife.

Angular piles of bones wrapped in leathery skin cropped up around camp. The first time I saw a mound of corpses in Buchenwald, I stood and scanned the pile in search of my father. Rats scurried among the tangle of limbs while feasting on the rotting flesh. The Germans worried the rodents might infect the soldiers with diseases, so they dumped the bodies in mass graves near the Bismarck Tower.

In March and early April, the word spread among the prisoners that liberation was near. Respected block leaders confirmed the reports, but rumors about Hitler's final plans for our extermination tempered our excitement. "The Germans are planning to drop bombs over Buchenwald. They will kill us off and destroy evidence of war crimes," I heard an older inmate say. "They will never let us make it out alive. We're all going to die if we don't mount an uprising."

"The camp is mined!" another warned. "They're going to blow us up minutes before the Americans arrive to free us!"

"I heard they have prisoners digging mass graves to bury us in," said another.

Everyone was frazzled and afraid. I didn't know whom or what to believe. All I knew was that I hadn't made it this far to be killed days or hours before regaining my freedom. I resolved to do whatever it took to stay alive.

In early April, prisoners swapped barracks, exchanged names with other prisoners, and wreaked all manner of havoc at night in an effort to confuse the soldiers at roll call. The idea was to run out the clock before the Nazis could march us off to mass graves. Then, on April 4, something happened that I never thought I'd see. We stiffened our spines. When the voice came over the loudspeakers ordering all Jews to report for roll call, not a single prisoner went. The underground resistance had determined that the Nazis planned to machine-gun Jews on the *Appelplatz*.

I expected the Nazis to inflict brutal punishment following the stand down. In a sense, they did. They stopped supplying our daily food rations and began evacuations two days later. But what I did not know—what only a handful of us knew—was that one of the underground prisoner organizations had forged a letter from the Americans and delivered it to the commandant of Buchenwald, Hermann Pister. The phony letter promised leniency for Pister if he delivered us to the Americans without inflicting further atrocities against us. Instead of gunning us down, Pister evacuated prisoners in waves.

I'd survived one death march. I refused to go on another. I learned there was a Czech barrack nearby. The Czechs let me mix in with them. On April 6, the Germans sent three thousand inmates marching out of Buchenwald. The next day seven thousand were evacuated. On April 9, nearly five thousand prisoners were sent on a transport, and over nine thousand left the next day.

All the activity reminded me of an earlier conversation with an older prisoner, who had pulled me aside and whispered in my ear. "You've worked in the munitions factory, yes?" he asked.

"Yes," I said.

"The underground needs a special weapons part from that facility," he said. "You are in that building. Perhaps you could get it."

I told him I knew nothing about weapons parts and probably wasn't the best person for the job, but I would look around and see what I could do. "I can't promise anything," I stressed.

"That's fine. Just look for it, and let us know if you see anything or know anyone who could get their hands on it."

I had heard about the underground prisoner resistance from older inmates but knew very few details. Word was that they had a cache of stolen German guns ready for a prisoner uprising.

⁓

April 11, 1945, was the day of my rebirth.

I awoke to the din of prisoners racing between barracks. "Get up! It's happening! Today is the day!" someone said. I crawled out of my sleeping rack and bounded to the floor before pulling on my prisoner pants and wooden shoes. I huddled behind the other prisoners peering out our barrack doors.

Buchenwald was bedlam. Prisoners were running in every direction as the remaining German soldiers scrambled to prepare their retreat. Commandant Pister and many other SS had already fled. Around ten o'clock a voice over the loudspeaker ordered, "All members of the SS leave the camp immediately!"

A roar rolled through the barracks. Members of the underground prisoner resistance frantically handed out the modest collection of smuggled machine guns and weapons to block elders, and the children were ordered to stay inside the barracks. We found out later that a Russian officer and fellow prisoner had organized the uprising that took the SS officers off the watchtower and helped free us.

Around eleven o'clock on the morning of the eleventh, we heard the sweet sounds of tanks from General George S. Patton's Third Army pummeling the Nazis in the distance. The blasts grew louder and louder, our hearts fuller and fuller.

I walked to the barrack door and looked out at the frenetic blur. Nazis ran in search of a life-saving change of clothes—clothes that would camouflage their bestial depravity. A well-known and dedicated SS sadist sprinted past me wearing a Russian uniform he'd raided from a Russian POW. Other soldiers shot prisoners for the striped wardrobe of oppression they made us wear. They hoped the rags would spare them from the gallows as war criminals.

The shirt! I said to myself. I ran back to my rack and took off the soldier's shirt I'd worn religiously under my striped prisoner uniform. The shirt had now lost its power. Not even the Nazis would wear it.

I could hear the American tanks rumble as the concussions from the gun blasts echoed off the barrack walls. Nazi machine guns returned fire. I sat in my rack and prayed a simple prayer. "God, please let the Americans win. Please, God. Please," I prayed.

God answered my prayer around 2:30 that afternoon. The American tanks from the Sixth Armored Division reached the SS military barracks. At precisely 3:15 p.m., the white flag of surrender flew over Buchenwald. Ours was the first camp the Americans liberated. But the euphoric cries ringing across Buchenwald were muted by the extreme hunger we were suffering after nearly six days without food.

Roughly twenty-one thousand prisoners remained on liberation day. Eight hundred fifty of them were children like Elie Wiesel and me. I remember seeing Elie at Buchenwald and thinking he was the skinniest kid I ever saw. I was a bag of bones, too. But at least we were teenagers. When the Americans arrived to take care of us children, to their utter shock, they found among the inmates a three-year-old boy.

Food came quickly. So did the sickness. Our emaciated bodies and withered organs couldn't handle the shock of food. People became severely ill from eating too much too fast. The American doctors examined my symptoms, tended my wounds, and placed me on a special diet designed for my smaller frame. Whatever the Americans told me to eat, I ate. Whatever they said to avoid, I avoided. I trusted them completely. How could I not? They were Americans. They saved me.

Peace and gratitude came over me the minute I laid eyes on the American soldiers. The skeletons and stench mortified the GIs. I couldn't take my eyes off them. Their uniforms, their composure, their compassion—I loved them, wanted to be one of them.

The next day, April 12, my future client and hero forever, Supreme Allied Commander General Dwight D. Eisenhower, rolled into Buchenwald at the nearby subcamp of Ohrdruf near Gotha. Eisenhower was ten feet tall in my mind. He is still. Ike brought General Omar Bradley and General George S. Patton along with him to see the nightmare firsthand. They saw the starved prisoners hobbling on pipe-stem legs. They saw the bodies charred on Ohrdruf's pyre. They unlatched a door and surveyed a room stacked high with rotting corpses. Actually, that was one sight General Patton did not see. As Eisenhower wrote to General George Marshall a few days later:

> The things I saw beggar description.... The visual evidence and the verbal testimony of starvation, cruelty and bestiality were so overpowering as to leave me a bit sick. In one room, where [there] were piled up twenty to thirty naked men, killed by starvation, George Patton would not even enter. He said he would get sick if he did so. I made the visit deliberately, in order to be in a position to give *first hand* evidence of these things if ever, in the future, there develops a tendency to charge these allegations merely to "propaganda."

Ike toured the human ruins. He ordered every soldier in the area not on the front lines to do the same. "We are told that the American soldier does not know what he is fighting for," said Eisenhower. "Now, at least, he will know what he is fighting *against*." During his walk through the camp, Eisenhower turned to a GI and said, "Still having trouble hating [the Nazis]?"

Later, Patton informed Ike that the mayor of Gotha and his wife hanged themselves after touring the Ohrdruf concentration camp. "Maybe there is hope after all," quipped Eisenhower.

Wisely, the general displayed Buchenwald to the world. He designed an aggressive publicity offensive to prevent the Germans and others from averting their eyes in denial. Soon the Americans had German civilians touring the camps, smelling the bodies, walking through the death chambers, and digging mass graves to bury the Shoah dead.

The Germans touring Buchenwald looked at us like zoo animals. Some women bore pained faces and shed tears. Others held their hands over their mouths and noses to guard themselves from breathing in our stench and germs. Many Germans feigned shock and surprise at the mounds of corpses that piled up when the crematoria ran out of coal. And perhaps some genuinely were surprised by the *depths* of depravity to which the SS had descended. But I will go to my grave believing that the many who lived in and around the camps knew what Hitler and his henchmen were up to. How could they not? From 1933 to 1945, Nazi Germany created twenty thousand camps of all kinds, including transit camps, forced-labor camps, and extermination camps. Companies bought us as slave labor. We were hauled in trains across the countryside. We were beaten and killed on labor sites outside the camps. And it took tens of thousands of Nazis to run the death machine—tens of thousands of Nazis who were genocidal monsters by day, family men by night. By 1945, 6,297 members of the SS and 532 female guards worked at Buchenwald alone.

Trust me. People knew.

In the days after liberation, I pondered these enraging facts. I desperately wanted to heal my body and locate my family. But my spirit needed mending too. When the Americans announced a U.S. Army chaplain would perform the first Jewish religious ceremony inside Buchenwald, I attended.

On April 20, 1945, Rabbi Herschel Schacter conducted the first Friday night Sabbath service. There was singing, reciting of blessings, prayer, and much weeping. It was moving. Yet all through the service the question I could not escape that night on the Death March to Gleiwitz haunted me still.

The next day Rabbi Schacter was mulling about outside the Czech barracks. In Yiddish he said, "Is there a Jew around here who can speak Yiddish?"

"I can," I said in Yiddish.

"Thank you," he said. "Where are the Jews around here?"

"This is the Czech barracks," I told him. "I'm one of the few Jews here. They let me stay here because I'm from Czechoslovakia."

"I see," he said.

"Rabbi, I attended your service last night. It was very beautiful. But may I please ask you a question?"

"Of course," he said.

"Rabbi, I must know: Where was God?"

He stood still and silent.

"Look what happened!" I pleaded. "Where was God? Where?"

"There are no answers to certain questions," he said staring off in the distance. "That is a question for which there is no answer." I lowered my head and cried. Rabbi Schacter wrapped his arms around me and held me.

~

Not everyone who was alive the day the Americans rolled into camp lived to tell about it. Five days after liberation, the Americans counted the prisoners again. Despite the Allies' heroic military and medical relief efforts, a thousand prisoners had already died. I still think about them, people who touched but could not clasp freedom.

Today the Buchenwald clock tower's hands are permanently set to 3:15, the time of our liberation. But what of those who met their fate just moments prior? Like the men who died on the death marches when the Nazis evacuated Buchenwald days before. Or the prisoners whom the Nazis shot for their striped uniforms only hours before the Americans arrived. Or the infirmed who died in the racks minutes before liberation's dawn. They died in that shadowless moment just beyond the speed of grace. They died as terror's last eyewitnesses.

To have been so close, to have persevered so much, to have escaped the gas and the guns and the ovens, yet never to have been granted the chance to live free—I cry for them.

I cry for the six million innocents who died in the clutch of darkness without warrant or repose.

I cry for Mother.

I cry for Father.

I cry for Grandmother Geitel.

I cry for Grandfather Abraham.

I cry for Simcha.

I cry for Rivka.

I cry for the baby, Sruel Baer.

I cry.

CHAPTER FIVE

A TIME TO KILL

P hysically, I was free. Emotionally, I was in chains.

The SS at Buchenwald had surrendered and fled. The German army had not. That meant we were free to leave and reenter the camp as we pleased, but our safety was far from certain.

The Allies brought in caring people and organizations to help us piece together our shattered lives. But I couldn't get my mind off the mayor's wife. I couldn't let go of my rage and lust for revenge. I'd made a promise to myself. And I intended to keep it. I would return to Weimar and kill her.

I located two Jewish boys who were well enough to make the walk to Weimar. I told them what the woman did and what I was prepared to do about it. We could rummage machine guns from the mountain of German weapons seized by the inmates and Americans that lay in piles on the *Appelplatz*. The boys vowed solidarity. Having survived hell, they too were eager to see justice administered.

We left Buchenwald on foot and set out toward Weimar. The newfound freedom was odd and unsettling. No longer were marches marked by insults, beatings, and killings. Indeed, we were not "marching" at all but walking, and of our own accord. The transition from slave back to civilian disoriented me. Captivity had made freedom feel disorderly, vulnerable. Even simple things, like hearing someone call your name instead of a number, took some getting used to.

The streets outside camp were electric with an ominous sense of disquiet. A smattering of prisoners in striped pajamas ambled in search of noncamp food. I kept my eyes open for SS. We gripped our guns and got to Weimar as quickly as possible.

None of us had ever fired a machine gun. I knew my way around a basic pistol from my father's training before he tried to hide me in the forest. This gun, however, was a different matter.

My heartbeat quickened the closer we got to the mayor's house. Pent-up rage from all I had seen and experienced surged through me. Killing the mayor's wife could not repay the Nazis for the terror they had inflicted on us. But it was a start.

We walked a few miles before turning down the street the mayor's home was on. I pointed to a house several paces down the road: "I think that's it." The big black Mercedes was not out front. It took me a moment to make sure I had the right house.

"You sure this is it?" one of the boys asked.

"Yes, I'm sure."

"What's the plan?" the other boy asked.

"The car isn't here. Looks like the house is empty," I said. "The plan is we take our guns and go in through the side door. Then we hide and wait so I can kill the blond bitch that had me beaten."

The boys nodded.

"Okay, let's go," I said.

We crept up to the side door. I slowly turned the knob. It was unlocked. I entered the house quietly, with my gun drawn. The boys fell in behind me and eased the door shut. We stepped softly to mute the sounds of our wooden clogs on the floor.

"Hello?" a voice around a corner said. "Hello?"

Just then the beautiful blond woman turned the corner and let out a screech. She had the baby in her arms again.

"Don't shoot!" she screamed. "Don't shoot!"

"Remember me?!" I yelled. "Do you?!"

Her blond tresses shook violently. She hid her face behind her upraised hand as if shielding herself from the sun.

"You had me beaten because of the rabbits. I'm here to shoot you!" I said, sounding like an SS.

"No! Please!" she quavered. "The baby, please!"

I aimed the machine gun at her chest. The baby wailed. My finger hovered above the trigger.

"Shoot her!" one of the boys said. "Shoot her!" The woman's outstretched hand trembled in the air. My heart pounded against my chest like a hammer.

"Shoot her!" the other boy yelled. "That's what we came here for! Do it!"

I froze. I couldn't do it. I could not pull the trigger. That was the moment I became human again. All the old teachings came rushing back. I had been raised to believe that life was a precious gift from God, that women and children must be protected. Had I pulled the trigger, I would have been like Mengele. He too had faced mothers holding babies—*my* mother holding *my* baby brother—and sentenced both to gruesome deaths. My moral upbringing would not allow me to become an honorary member of the SS.

Still, extending mercy felt weak. I tried to save face in front of the boys. If I couldn't be a hardened killer, I could at least be a car thief. "Where is the car?" I yelled.

"There is nothing," she said.

"Where is it?!" I barked.

"It's not here," she said.

I lowered the gun and stomped out of the house and went around back.

"You made us come here for nothing?" one of the boys huffed.

"I couldn't shoot her," I said. "She had a baby!"

"How many babies did *they* kill?" he retorted. He had a point.

We walked to the large barn behind the house and unlatched the heavy wooden doors. There, covered with hay, sat the big black Mercedes. "That lying Nazi bitch!" one of the boys yelled. I was livid. I'd spared her life and she lied to my face.

"Wait here," I told the boys. I marched back in the house, gun drawn, and found her. "This time I'm really going to shoot you," I said. "Give me the keys!" She gave me the keys. I jogged back to the boys and the car. "I got them," I said, rattling the keys in my hand.

"Who knows how to drive?" one of the boys asked.

"Don't worry, I do," I said. We brushed off the hay and hopped in the car.

"Hurry up! Let's get out of here," one of the boys said.

I set my machine gun on the floorboard and slid the key into the ignition. I was a little rusty but knew how to drive from my auto mechanic days in Budapest. The big German engine cranked loud and strong. I pulled out of the Weimar mayor's mansion driveway and punched the gas.

What a sight we must have been: three teenage Jews in striped prisoner uniforms, armed with machine guns, driving a black Mercedes in Weimar, Germany, on our way back to the Buchenwald concentration camp. We smiled, laughed, and talked tough like the men we weren't.

"Did you see how scared she was?" one boy said excitedly. "I bet she made in her underwear!" We chuckled and drove on.

"Look!" one of the boys said pointing out the window. "Two girls!" I pulled the car to the side of the street.

We invited the German girls to take a ride. They must have been so mesmerized by the Mercedes that our raggedy uniforms failed to give them pause. To my surprise, they hopped in. This was the closest any of us had been to attractive girls in a long, long time. They rode with us a few blocks before we dropped them off.

I contemplated ditching the car. After all, we were driving the mayor of Weimar's Mercedes. If that didn't give us away, the license plates would. But then I thought, *What the hell? When's the next time you will get to drive a Mercedes?* So I drove the car all the way back to Buchenwald. In fact, I drove straight through the camp gates. Today, the irony of the slogan emblazoned across the gates—"To each what he deserves"—makes me laugh.

Prisoners stood motionless and stared as we coasted into camp. They must have assumed an important dignitary or the mayor of

Weimar himself would step out of the fancy car. When they saw our striped prisoner uniforms, they rushed us. "How did you get a Mercedes?" someone asked.

"Well," I said smiling, "we just got it."

Later I noticed a prisoner on a motorbike with a sidecar eyeing my big black Mercedes. I liked his bike. He liked my car. I told him we should trade. He agreed. He taught me how to crank the motorbike and unhook the sidecar. I rode my new motorbike over to the Czech barracks and parked it outside. For weeks I drove anyone who wanted a ride in and out of camp. Fine piece of German engineering, that bike.

⁓

The war came to a close on April 30, 1945, when a broken, desperate Adolf Hitler committed suicide by gunshot in his Berlin bunker. A week later the German army surrendered. I was grateful to be alive but anxious about my future. We all were. Our lives were in limbo. Going "home" was not an option for most. Hatred of Jews remained high. Everything we owned had been seized and stolen. Millions of our relatives had been murdered. I didn't know what lay in store. I didn't really care. My singular obsession was living free and finding my phantom family. Nothing would stand in my way.

In May, Czechoslovakia sent officials to Buchenwald to retrieve its citizens. They boarded us on a bus and drove us to Prague, the capital of Czechoslovakia.

The Allies and the United Nations had set up displaced persons (DP) camps and other places of refuge throughout Germany, Italy, Austria, and elsewhere to take in the nearly quarter of a million displaced Jews. There you could sleep, eat, connect with fellow Jews, and receive educational training and relocation support. HIAS (which originally stood for the Hebrew Immigrant Aid Society) also held Jewish gatherings where you always felt safe and welcome.

You can keep a vigilant eye on the DP camps' survivor lists and photo bulletins, I thought. *You can check them any time and use the DP camps as a place to land when needed. Same goes for HIAS. You can depend on them for help. Why not get well and start looking for my family?*

The bus ride from Buchenwald to Prague felt surreal. I stared out the window and watched the German towns and countryside race past my face and recede from my mind. I had to make a mental break. I had to bury the childhood innocence that died an agonizing death in Auschwitz, Buna, Gleiwitz, and Buchenwald. I was sixteen. I had seen more death and destruction than a hundred civilian men combined. My father had told me if I survived I must honor our family, not by feeling guilty, but by living life to the fullest. I would not disobey Father. In fact, I did him one better: I signed up to fight the tyranny that had taken my family from me.

We stepped off the bus at Prague and experienced a registration line far different from the ones the Nazis administered. Instead of shaving our heads and stealing our clothes, they gave us medical attention and plenty of civilian food. I had processing papers from the Buchenwald camp but chose not to show them. Instead, I told the registrars I was eighteen years old and wanted to enlist in the Czechoslovakian army. They were unwilling to take me when they saw my weakened condition. But after I had rested and healed in the local sanitarium for several weeks, I was signed up and shipped off for a couple months of basic training. The army issued me a uniform. The fabric, the styling, the angular military cut and silhouette—I beamed every time I wore it. It made me look and feel like a man, like someone my family would be proud to call their son. I had finally reached that moment of maturity every boy passes through on the way to adulthood when he embraces, not rejects, wearing a suit. You can always tell when a boy has reached manhood by the clothes hanging in his closet.

I liked wearing a suit so much I decided I needed a civilian suit or two of my own. On one occasion our unit was sent on a quick mission to Germany. During the trip we stumbled upon a textile warehouse packed with bolts of fabric. I knew nothing about weave and thread counts, so I chose four large cuts that looked handsome and felt nice between my fingers. When we returned to Czechoslovakia, I took the four pieces of fabric to a tailor in the city. I told him I would give him two cuts of cloth if he would take the other two and make me two suits. He agreed, measured me up, and made me two simple suits. I was building a young man's beginner wardrobe. For what, I wasn't sure. But if I'd learned anything in the camps, I'd learned that what you wore could change your life.

The war effort was dying down, and the army discharged me after a few short months of service. They let me keep my uniform. I was proud of that uniform and to have served my country in it. But it proved useful on another level as well. Every time I traveled and wore my uniform, girls noticed it. More importantly, Russian soldiers respected it—not me, but the suit and what it represented.

Following my stint in the Czech army, I felt entrepreneurial and homesick. I wanted to earn my own money, to travel, and to find my family.

I frantically sought news of my family in Budapest and Romania, never giving up hope. I had heard so many horror stories of other families separated in the camps never to see each other again that optimism became nearly impossible.

With an increasingly heavy heart, I searched.

My quest to find my father ended the summer of 1946 in Budapest.

For some reason, I always felt that if I ever found my father alive, it would be in Hungary. I made a special effort to register my father's name at HIAS gatherings when traveling there. But that ended when I ran into a man named Mendel.

I knew Mendel before the Shoah. He lived near my hometown of Pavlovo. When I stopped at a Hungarian HIAS location, Mendel and I exchanged pleasantries. He then shared the news that changed the trajectory of my life.

"What are you doing here?" asked Mendel.

"Oh, I thought I would check the name lists and photo bulletins," I said. "I do that everywhere I go. Look, look, look! That's all I do it seems," I smiled to mask the hurt.

"I don't understand what you mean," he said. The confused look on his face made me uncomfortable.

"My father—I haven't found him yet. If he's alive I want to know where he is," I insisted. Mendel's apparent obtuseness made me angry. Surely I wasn't the first survivor he'd spoken to who was looking for a loved one. Mendel's face grew serious and somber.

"You can stop looking," he said. "I was there the day the Germans shot him."

"What?!"

"I'm so sorry to have to be the one to tell you this. I was there. You can stop looking," he said. He could see that I was about to faint. "Sit down," he said.

I sat down.

"Your father was a special man. He loved you very much," said Mendel.

I wept.

"Joseph was in charge of directing a building project. It was a small bridge. I was there on the worksite. We didn't finish construction on deadline. So the Nazis shot him. I saw it happen," he said.

I put my face in my hands and cried. My heart hurt—physically *hurt*. Mendel put his hand on my shoulder and tried to console me.

"Maxi, I'm so very sorry," he said. "But crying isn't going to bring him back. You have to do what he would have wanted you to do. You have to be a man, make your own way now."

"What camp were you two in?" I asked Mendel.

"Buchenwald."

"*Buchenwald?* I was in Buchenwald!" I said frantically. "When did they shoot my father?" Mendel looked away as if he wished I hadn't asked that question. "I have to know," I urged. "Please. When?"

"About one week before the liberation," he said softly.

I buried my face in my hands again. I shut my eyes tight and tears streamed down my forearms. I drew inside myself, consumed by a wave of despair that left me dizzy. At that moment I would have relived the horror of the Death March and the beatings a hundred times to have five minutes with my father, to tell him how much I loved him. Mendel was still speaking, offering words of counsel, but I had stopped listening. I think I always knew this day would come—that one day I would have to hold my father's funeral in my heart. But I was unprepared to hear it this way. Knowing the timing made the ache all the deeper.

One week *from liberation!* I thought. *He came so close. He almost made it!*

I don't remember much about my parting with Mendel or where I went afterward. Just that my first fears were confirmed— I was all alone in the world. The father I loved, the man who gave me everything I needed and taught me honor and integrity, murdered and gone.

Death from illness or an act of nature I could have handled. Not willful murder based on blood and belief. Not a slaying over lineage and faith. The execution's moral grotesqueness and the loss of my hero ripped a hole in my heart that remains to this day. Sometimes at night when I dream, he comes to me, strong and smiling. He tells me he's proud of me and loves me. Would that I could live inside those dreams forever.

In a daze, I headed back to Prague, where I could be around survivors who spoke Yiddish and had endured similar horrors. Their presence made me feel a little less broken. My father and mother and siblings would have insisted that I stay strong, so I thought of ways that I could honor their memories and move forward. My time there started to ease the pain—though of course that would never go away—and stoked my entrepreneurial fires. I talked to the other boys and men about their future plans and past businesses. I liked the idea of starting from scratch. I wanted to build something myself that could produce pride and a profit. An older man at the camp told me he had owned his own store before the Shoah. The easiest way to learn business, he said, was to buy things people want at a good price and then resell them for a little more. "How do you know what people want to buy?" I asked.

"Easy," he said. "People want whatever they can't or don't have."

The next day I rounded up a half dozen boys my age to launch my foray into the import-export business. "There is no use sitting around and waiting for things to happen," I said passionately. "We need to make things happen." I then imparted my deep business knowledge of supply and demand. "We can earn money by giving people the things they want but can't or don't have," I said, as if I were the first person to ever have the idea.

The plan was to buy cigarettes and distribute them to buyers in hard-to-reach cities who would pay a slight premium for our professional delivery services. Then I sweetened my sales pitch. Working in two-man teams, we would split any profits equally among ourselves. We'd travel, meet girls—maybe even find our surviving relatives. "All we need to do is start!" I exclaimed to the group of increasingly excited boys. The pitch worked.

"Where should we start?" one boy asked.

"We should start in Budapest," I said. "I know the area and some people." So we rode the train to Budapest, but not on the inside. Because we couldn't afford tickets, we sneaked aboard and rode the top. For a time, "train hopping" became our primary means of transportation.

Returning to Budapest was bittersweet. I located the nearest HIAS gathering to get the latest update on my family members and to ask around for any information that would help me locate them. No one knew or had heard anything about them.

I then found the man who had hired me as an auto mechanic in my youth. He remembered and greeted me warmly. He said the girls at the brothel had all moved on. That made me happy. I asked him if I could work a couple days to earn a little cash for our new business venture. He liked the idea and even agreed to introduce me to a few people who might be interested in our services.

That became our routine: Work an odd job for a few days as laborers, earn some capital, and identify a bargain-price vendor. We then made two-man runs by train and resold the cigarettes. After several weeks we had built up a nice little business that allowed us to purchase a ticket and ride *inside* the train instead of on top.

In Budapest I mustered the courage to make a one-day trip to my hometown of Pavlovo. I was nervous about going. Anxious thoughts floated through my mind: *Would my home still be standing? Would the townspeople have information on my family's whereabouts? Had any of my family members already been by the house to see if I'd returned home in search of them?*

When I got to my house, Russians had taken it over. I could not bring myself to knock on the door. I wanted to remember it the way it existed in my heart and mind. I couldn't bear the thought of seeing Soviet Communist gear strewn about the place where we had made so many family memories together.

I walked past my home and went to the cemetery where our relatives were buried. I prayed a simple prayer and left. I never wanted to go there ever again. I told myself that I needed to find my family.

Maybe they're sick and in a hospital somewhere. Or maybe they are looking for me and we just haven't run into one another yet.

Hope's grip on me was intense—and futile. But the hope made the living possible, so I used it as an incentive and returned to Budapest to resume making cigarette train runs.

One sales trip to Prague was particularly memorable. One of the boys named Willie and I secured a suitcase of cigarettes and two bottles of vodka. Our plan was to carry them by train to Prague to sell them for a profit. The biggest obstacles we encountered were the Russian soldiers, who were notorious for shaking down easy targets. We sat in a train compartment and placed our bags near our feet, tying the bags to our legs with string to prevent robbers from stealing our inventory when we dozed off. About halfway through the train ride, a uniformed Russian soldier approached us and sat in our compartment. He seemed friendly enough at first, so I gave him some vodka. Within an hour, though, he was drunk and verbally abusive, hurling anti-Semitic slurs at us and threatening to have us imprisoned.

I snapped.

I grabbed his sidearm and hit him over the head with it, knocking him out cold. "Hurry up," I told Willie. "Help me get his uniform off."

My traveling companion was scared to death. We skivvied off the soldier's jacket. I put it on. Instantly, I became a Russian soldier. My friend was beside himself. We slid the Russian down on the ground and shoved him under the seat bench inside the compartment. I sat in his vacant seat and pretended to be him. When someone saluted me, I saluted back. The uniform's power amazed me.

"We have to jump off this train," Willie pleaded. "They're going to find out what we did." We slid the Russian out from under the bench. My friend re-dressed him while I put my clothes back on. Every time the soldier stirred, I knocked him out again.

Back at our makeshift home base, we met four Jewish girls. They, like us, were survivors and parentless. They gave me hope that, however improbably, some young girls—girls like my sisters—had survived the Shoah. By now I knew that going to the left at Auschwitz meant being gassed and burned in the ovens. Still, the girls' presence lifted my hopes.

We bragged to the girls about our booming import-export business and said they should travel with us so we could keep them safe. That wasn't just a pick-up line. Russian soldiers were notorious for raping girls traveling alone on trains. We had heard it happen several times even in broad daylight. The Russians didn't care. The screaming, the struggling—it was horrible. We would not let our girls be traumatized yet again.

Protecting our girls felt good. They were fun and sweet. We would flirt, kiss, and distract one another from our grim reality. To us, life was an adventure. We weren't afraid to take risks. What did we have to lose that we hadn't lost already? We were poor but proud. When something good happened for one of us, we shared the spoils. Like the time one of the boys in our group secured a calf from a farm. That night we made a family feast. I knew how to skin and butcher a calf from my days in Pavlovo, and the girls knew how to cook it. We dined like kings and queens and thought it the best veal money could buy.

One of the girls in our group was named Magda. She and I shared a birthday and a hometown, and I felt a certain kinship with her. On one train ride, I saw a Russian soldier take a liking to Magda. Another boy from our group nudged me and snapped his head over in their direction. We stared intently and watched them talk. The Russian seemed sincere. We walked over to assess the situation.

Magda's eyes let me know she felt uncomfortable, that the Russian was coming on too strong and that she needed help. We engaged in small talk for a while. The Russian proceeded to declare his undying love for Magda, a total stranger he had only met a couple of hours before.

"That's wonderful," I said. "When we arrive you can meet Magda's father and mother and ask for her hand in marriage," I joked. The Russian didn't get the joke.

"That would be lovely," he said. "I'd like that very much." Magda shot me dagger eyes. I knew the train system extremely well. When the train stopped, we ditched the Russian Romeo and never saw him again.

Business was humming. Even though selling cigarettes out of suitcases was not my long-term goal, I was young and free again. I was also in my home country of Czechoslovakia, based in a camp at Teplice-Sanov. The connection to my roots felt good, kept me grounded, and drew my focus away from news of my father's death.

That is, until the Russian Communists began making their moves on Czechoslovakia. You must remember that during this time Czechoslovakia was the last democratic country in Eastern Europe. We even had good relations with the Russians because they had liberated us. But things were changing—and fast. Communists had infiltrated top government posts and were making rapid gains. I had seen the slow creep of evil once before. I wasn't about to stick around to see my freedom and property die a second death. Sharing with one's neighbors out of free choice was one's right. But government seizure of one's wages and property for the purposes of redistribution of wealth at the barrel of a gun was tyranny. I wanted none of it.

As much as it pained me to do so, I made plans in the fall of 1946 to leave my homeland to escape the looming Soviet takeover. As it turned out, I planned my exodus at just the right time. In the May 1946 elections, the Communists won 38 percent of the vote. In 1948, Czechoslovakia fell into forty years of deadly Communist rule.

My plan was simple: pack the few things I owned and run away. Specifically, I would try to sneak across the Czech-German border and get to the large Gabersee DP camp near Wasserberg, Germany, located in the American occupation zone. I felt safe with the Americans. The trouble was sneaking back into the country responsible for murdering my family. The first time I tried to enter Germany, the German border guards stopped me. I got testy with the officer. When he grabbed my arm to escort me away, I became unhinged and caused a spectacle.

"You cannot touch me! Never again!" I hollered at the top of my lungs. "Shoot me, but do not touch me. Never again can you touch me! No German will ever arrest me again!" The German officer was stunned.

That night I slept in Czechoslovakia near the border. The next evening I successfully snuck into Germany by running through the forest. I headed straight to the relatively new Gabersee DP camp. I made the camp my home. Speaking with the older Jewish men about religion and Israel reinvigorated my faith. I realized God must have a plan for my life, a reason for saving me from the ovens. I contemplated traveling to Israel to find my extended relatives, and joining the *Aliyah Bet*, the clandestine operation to smuggle persecuted Jews into Palestine. I even joined a *kibbutz*, a Jewish agrarian commune. It didn't go so well. When they told me we had to share everything with each other, including our clothes, I protested. "No, I don't share my clothes with anybody!" I told them. They made a special exception and allowed me to keep and wear my own clothes. Still, the fit wasn't right. I was too stubborn and independent to make a good *kibbutznik*.

I was seeking God, yearning for an answer to the questions I had asked Rabbi Schacter at Buchenwald: Where was God? How could He love me and let me go through such pain and loss?

Throughout my life I had heard that everything happens for a reason, that God's ways were mysterious but purposeful. I believed that. But something I read decades after my showdown at the mayor of Weimar's house proved to me that in the end, in this life or the one after, God ultimately achieves justice. A friend shared with me an article from a 1945 issue of *Life* magazine about Nazi suicides following the war. Here is a portion of what it said: "In the last days of the war the overwhelming realization of utter defeat was too much for many Germans. Stripped of the bayonets and bombast which had given them power, they could not face a reckoning with either their conquerors or their consciences. These found the quickest and surest escape in what Germans call *Selbstmord*, self-murder.... In Hitler's Reich, Germans stopped killing others and began killing themselves. In Weimar the mayor and his wife, after seeing Buchenwald atrocities, slashed their wrists."

That day at the mayor's home, God pricked my conscience. In so doing He spared me the guilt and shame of killing the mayor of Weimar's wife. I didn't need to kill her. She did it for me.

CHAPTER SIX

COMING TO AMERICA

Envisioning a future was an indulgence I had not allowed myself since my family's capture. Despite all odds, I had made friends and survived by running cigarettes. But the weight of my father's death prompted me to take a break from traveling and trading. The Gabersee DP camp in Wasserburg, Germany, became my home for six months. We played cards and soccer, met girls, and spent time getting to know new camp visitors. There were no work requirements. If you wanted to work, you worked. If you wanted to do nothing, you did nothing. I liked to work. My modestly successful business and expanding wardrobe boosted my self-confidence. At Auschwitz and Buchenwald, I'd worked thirteen-hour days without pay in deplorable conditions, interrupted only by the occasional beating. Now I worked because I wanted to. Better still, the government did not confiscate my possessions and the fruits of my labors. Earning and keeping my own money empowered me to help myself and others.

During my time off from black-market trading, I worked as a mechanic with the United Nations Relief and Rehabilitation Administration (UNRRA) area team's motor pool, maintaining engines and vehicles as needed. I always enjoyed the challenge of working with my hands and making things better than I found them.

Still, somewhere along the way I decided that military service to one's country was the surest pathway to manhood. That belief intensified after I learned of my father's murder. I wanted the discipline and camaraderie that came through service to something bigger than oneself. With my short run in the Czech army completed, I searched for another way to give back. Others had died on the battlefields and in the gas chambers. My conscience would not permit me to sit on the sidelines of history.

One day at Gabersee, an older Jewish man told me about the *Aliyah Bet*. The Hebrew word "Aliyah" means "immigration." "Bet" is the second letter of the Hebrew alphabet. The man explained to me that Jews were engaged in a covert "second immigration." The British, who controlled Palestine, had allied themselves with the Arabs to stop Holocaust survivors from going to the Jewish homeland. He said Jewish volunteers had launched a secret mission to smuggle Jewish refugees and survivors into Palestine. An underground network called the *Brihah* ("flight" in Hebrew) helped move Jews from DP camps in Germany, Austria, Italy, and elsewhere to port cities in places like Italy, France, and Greece. There, the refugees boarded boats bound for the homeland.

The Americans supported the effort and devoted 10 ships manned with 250 American veterans who had volunteered to help transport Jewish Holocaust survivors from Europe across the Mediterranean Sea. Holocaust survivors attempting to enter Palestine and intercepted by the British went to internment camps.

That was all I needed to hear. "How can I help?" I asked. The man smiled.

"Well," he said gently, "you're probably a little too young to help with something like this."

"I'm eighteen right now and will be nineteen in August. I served in the Czechoslovakian army. I survived the Nazis and the concentration camps. I can help," I said.

"What skills do you have?" he asked, only slightly less skeptical.

"I am an auto mechanic for the UNRRA motor pool," I said.

"Do you know how to drive?" he asked.

"Of course," I said. "I've driven all kinds of vehicles."

"What about a large truck?"

"Well, I haven't driven one of those yet," I confessed. "But I'm sure I can figure it out. Let me try."

He said an American Army officer who also spoke German was in charge of our area's *Aliyah* effort and that he would introduce me to him since I spoke and could understand German. "You mean Officer Taub?" I said. "I already know him. I see him at the motor pool from time to time. I didn't know he was involved in all this. I will talk to him."

A few days later, Taub and I discussed how I could be of service. Taub said I could start by driving the ambulance at the motor pool to get the feel of a bulkier vehicle. A few practice runs and I had the hang of it. Later he moved me up to larger trucks. Taub said after dark I was to take one of the motor pool's bigger vehicles. Then, between twenty and thirty men and women would pack themselves into the truck. I was to drive the transport toward Italy and drop the refugees off at predetermined locations.

"When you return," explained Taub, "the Americans overseeing the motor pool will arrest you and put you in jail for taking the truck. But don't worry. The next morning I will be there to get you out."

I made about a half-dozen human deliveries. Twice I got caught and had to spend the night in jail, just as Taub had warned. I didn't mind going to jail. A place to sleep hardly felt like punishment after a long night of driving. It was like a hotel—with bars. The following morning, Taub would swing by and spring me out of jail, just as he promised he would. Running Jews for the *Aliyah Bet* made me contemplate sneaking into Palestine myself. *What do you have to lose?* I thought. *At the very least you may find distant relatives, connect with your Jewish roots?*

As if in answer to the conversations I carried on in my head, a week or two later a man called Goldstein sent news of a letter from the United States waiting for me at my previous address. Despite my earlier unsavory dealings with the Russians, I returned to Teplice-Sanov and back without incident. The return address indicated the letter had been sent from a place in the United States I had never heard of before, "Baltimore, Maryland." I opened the envelope, which contained a letter written in Yiddish and an American one-dollar bill. It was from someone named Irving Berger, who claimed to be my maternal uncle.

While in the DP camps, I had never received mail from a family member. I eagerly read and reread the letter.

I wondered at first whether the mail carrier had me confused with another Maximilian Grünfeld. But the multiple references to names and events only a family member could know reassured me of the letter's authenticity. Oddly, Uncle Irving stated that he had included *ten* dollars. His generosity, it seems, had fallen victim to pilfering in the Russian mail. But it was the information in the letter, not the missing money, that intrigued me. Uncle Irving said my mother had never met him, or any of her other siblings, because she had been born much later, after her three sisters and two brothers had moved away. He said my mother's oldest sibling was a woman named Aunt Elka, who also lived in America, in a place called the Bronx of New York. Uncle Irving said I had another uncle, Antonio Berger, who lived in the neighboring country of Mexico. Each mention of a relative I never knew existed brought smiles and tears. It was miraculous that they had found me amid the chaos and carnage. They tried. They cared.

I was unforgotten.

Uncle Irving said I should come live in America. He said the family would gladly send me a ticket for the voyage. Questions flooded my mind.

How did he find me?

Should I forgo my plans to emigrate to the Jewish homeland?

Why should I make the hard journey to Palestine in the hopes of finding a relative when I have family in Baltimore, Maryland, and the Bronx, New York, already?

I should learn more about America. Eisenhower and the Americans liberated us. It's the least I can do.

Yes, I will read everything I can find. When I see "United States" written in the newspapers, I will read the article, even if I don't understand.

Wait... Officer Taub! He's a mentor to me. I will translate the letter for him tomorrow. He will teach me and tell me all about Baltimore, Maryland!

The next day, I accosted Taub at the motor pool. "Sir, I have several questions for you about America," I said excitedly in German. "May we speak a moment?"

"Sure," said Taub. "What do you want to know?"

"Well, you see, I got a letter. My first one ever from a family member in all my time in the camps. It says right here I have an Uncle Irving who lives in Baltimore, Maryland. What can you tell me about this place?"

"Great city," said the officer. "It's very close to many major places in America. It's not too far from the nation's capital, Washington, DC. It's also near two other big cities, Philadelphia and New York City."

"What are the people and government like there in those places? Communists? Nazis?"

The officer burst into laughter.

"No, no, no. None of that. It's freedom. That's America. It's a democratic government. The people decide."

"So, no concentration camps or anything like that?"

He chuckled and shook his head. "Try getting someone from Philly or New York in a concentration camp," he said with a smile. I nodded like I understood what he just said. "Where's this letter from your uncle?" Taub asked.

"It's right here," I said, holding up the envelope. "But it's written in Yiddish."

He took the envelope and looked at the return address.

"Read it to me and translate it for me," Taub said.

I read slowly to make sure I translated it as accurately as possible.

"What do you think?" I asked. "Should I go to America? Or should I take my chances with the *Aliyah Bet* and try to get to Palestine?"

"Don't even think of it," Taub said. "If your Uncle Irving sends you a ticket, go! You'll be happy. Trust me. There's no place like America."

"Yes, but what about Palestine?" I asked.

"What about Palestine? You don't even know if you have family there. According to what you just read from that letter, you have at least one aunt and one uncle in America, with another uncle just south of the border in Mexico. Why would you give up being with your family members when you might not even make it to Palestine?"

Taub confirmed what my heart already knew. I was grateful to have an older man I respected offer wisdom as I faced a life-altering decision. The fact he was an American clinched the decision.

"I can help you gather the necessary papers you would have to fill out to go to the U.S. as a refugee."

"Sir, I cannot thank you enough. I will do anything I have to. I want to learn all about America. I'm so excited," I said. "Thank you! Thank you!"

"Hold on now. You need to understand. It's a very, very long and complex process. The U.S. government has to approve you. That will take time," he said.

"I understand, I understand. I'm just so grateful that you would explain America to me. I just want a chance to be with my family," I said.

Learning about America and the faraway magical lands of Baltimore, Maryland, and the Bronx of New York became my obsessions. I carried the letter everywhere I went. I sent a reply to Uncle Irving at the address he included and thanked him for finding me. I said I would very much like to come to America to be with my family. We then began months of correspondence, each missive bringing me closer to my journey to America.

A few days later, Taub brought the stack of papers I needed to fill out to make my American voyage. I knew a little of what to expect from a friend I met at Gabersee, Kalvin Mermelstein. He was one of ten children, and his family were very close to my father. Even though all of his family members had survived the Shoah, Kalvin said he wanted a fresh start in America. He too had relatives in the United States, but he found that the extensive application could take months to process. Still, I had no idea how many hoops I would have to jump through to be considered for entry into America. I had to see a doctor, receive a battery of disease screenings, submit immunization records, undergo a background check, and provide documentation that I had an American sponsor who would take responsibility for me. I was happy to comply with all these legitimate and reasonable precautionary measures. But the volume and complexity of the paperwork made me worry that I might not be accepted.

Then one day at Gabersee I received notice from the United States government that my paperwork had been approved. I immediately wrote to Uncle Irving with the incredible news. He replied that he would send me clothes to wear for the passage and that I should watch for a ticket.

My cousin Mark Fendrich, Aunt Elka's son, purchased and mailed my ticket, which I received a few weeks later. The ticket made the possibility of a new life suddenly seem real. I would sail from Bremerhaven, Germany, aboard the SS *Ernie Pyle* on September 11, 1947. We would arrive seven days later in New York City. My ticket from Germany to America cost $142.

My days helping with the *Aliyah Bet* were over. America had accepted me. The family I desperately sought was an ocean away in the land of my liberators. The trip couldn't come soon enough.

As it turned out, the *Aliyah Bet*'s days were nearing an end as well. In July, an *Aliyah Bet* ship called the *Exodus 1947* left the French port of Sète carrying 4,515 Jewish men, women, and children. A week later, British troops boarded the ship—now just miles from Palestinian shores—sparking a deadly skirmish in which two passengers and a crewman were killed. The British shipped the passengers back to France, but the Jews refused to disembark. The French told the British they would not assist in forcibly removing them, so the British decided to send them back to Germany. The news that a ship full of Holocaust survivors was being sent back to the country that had tried to exterminate them provoked international condemnation. At the end of 1947, the United Nations voted to cut Palestine into two countries, one Jewish and the other Arab. On May 14, 1948, the modern state of Israel was born.

I arrived at Bremerhaven on the day of departure carrying a small bag that held all my possessions. Standing dockside I stared down the length of the 522-foot wall of riveted metal. I had never seen anything like it. The *Ernie Pyle*, named after the legendary American journalist, was a military cargo ship. At 14,600 tons, it was among the largest cargo ships in the United States Maritime Commission's entire fleet. I was impressed and anxious.

I stepped onto the ship and scanned the numerous smiling American soldiers happy to be headed home. I couldn't understand their words, but their friendly countenances put me at ease. We all lined up along the metal railings as the ship moved out of the harbor. People waved goodbye. I did not. Instead I stood with my arms resting on the metal rails and stared at Germany as we drifted away from it. Even after the others had waved their last goodbyes and blown their last kisses into the air, I stared. That German landmass, receding with each wave our ship sliced through, would forever be the keeper of my family's blood and ashes. As I took one long final look at the fading shoreline, I recalled my father's final words to me on our last night together in Auschwitz: "Honor us by living, by not feeling sorry for us. That is what you must do."

I won't let you down, Father, I promised him. *I'm going to do as you wished. I'm going to live a hope-filled and hardworking life, a life with enough happiness to fill the years each one of you lost. You watch, Father. I will do this. I will make you proud of me.*

I pushed myself up off the metal rail and looked each way. The crowds had long since dispersed to their cabins. I turned and smiled on my way to room C-40.

In addition to all the American soldiers on the ship, clusters of Jewish and German passengers made the voyage. I decided to join a group of Jewish men in a game of poker. I had developed an unhealthy confidence in my card-playing skills during countless card games in the DP camps. After a few hands with these men, I went looking for the only two people I knew on the boat. I'd met one of them, Danny Freid, at Gabersee. The other, a girl named Sylvia, I had first met in Teplice-Sanov. She was a little younger than I and had dark brown hair and a sweet disposition. Our paths had crossed on several occasions, but we were never more than friends. I found Danny but did not see Sylvia during the entire boat ride to America.

The first night on the *Ernie Pyle* proved to be my only good night of rest on the week-long voyage. The next morning I was so seasick I could barely get out of bed. Worse, the ocean currents had grown dramatically rougher overnight. The farther we sailed, the worse it got.

On day three of the trip, I forced myself to stumble out of my room and up to one of the top decks to get some fresh air. I wore one of the suit jackets the tailor had made for me in Prague. I looked out over the whitecaps cresting across the chop. Geysers of sea spray misted my face as waves slammed starboard. The cool water and blasts of air helped clear my head. The wind blew my coat back like a cape. I crossed my arms and gripped the lapels to keep the coat from flapping in the wind. When my legs got wobbly, I slid down against the wall and sat. Less than an hour later, a German girl a little older than I wandered out onto the deck. She looked green too. "Seasick?" I asked in German.

"Yes. I feel awful!" she said.

"Me too. The fresh air and being able to see the ocean is helping, though. Come join me," I said patting the space beside me. She slumped down on the deck. We sat in a comfortable silence for several minutes before the ship got hammered by deep and rolling waves that sent us sliding on the water-slick deck.

I pulled myself up to take a look over the railing. We had now entered a stretch of tall dark-blue waves that looked like deep craters. The ship's heavy bow dove down to the trough, shooting back up like a cork, only to dive again when it hit the crest. Down and up, down and up. "These waves are massive," I yelled. "Hold on." I crawled to a nearby coil of rope and tied one end to something heavy. I knelt beside the girl, looped the rope around both our waists and tied it off. "Just in case," I yelled.

She smiled, partly because it was funny and partly because she knew I was flirting. "Very creative," she said with a raised eyebrow. We were green-faced and wet, but we enjoyed each other's company. "Where are you going in America?" she asked.

"The Baltimore, Maryland," I said. "I also may visit the Bronx, New York." She looked confused but was too sick and tired to untangle my meaning. "My Uncle Irving lives in the Baltimore. He's the one who invited me to the United States of America. He wrote and said he is going to pick me up when we get there. I'm going to live with him to start. He's going to find me a job. I also wrote my friend, Kalvin Mermelstein, and told him to meet me at the dock. He came to America three months ago," I said. She nodded and smiled softly as I rambled. "What do you know about America?" I asked her over the loud and whipping winds.

"Big," she said stretching her arms and hands wide. "Very, very big."

We leaned against each other and closed our eyes to steal back a few minutes of repose from our lonely, restless nights. Sleeping against her felt peaceful. I awoke to the girl tapping me gently. "I need to go," she said. "Can you please untie me?" I loosened the rope knot from our waists.

"Maybe I will see you later," she said. "Hope you get well."

"Hope you feel better, too," I said.

Despite five consecutive days and nights of seasickness, nothing could dampen my excitement to reach America. I didn't know what to expect. My only real impressions of the United States had been formed through my interactions with American soldiers—all of which were positive. Eisenhower and his men saved and liberated me, Taub guided and counseled me, my uncle found me and invited me to live with him (in sharp contrast to my father's cousin in Budapest), my cousin generously provided for my passage. The Americans I had encountered displayed a generous and sacrificial spirit that made a lasting impression on me. I was headed to a place quite different from the European lands I knew.

The seas would not relent. The ride remained rough, but by the sixth day my body was getting used to the pounding. I could walk without feeling lightheaded. Most important, I could hold down food. That evening I made my way back to the poker tables with seven dollars in my pocket. I felt lucky. I was confident I could make much more. I stood and watched the players for a while before working my way into a table. After several hands, we had a big pot going. I had a full house: three kings and two aces. *This is your shot,* I thought. *No one can beat you. You have to go for it.* I went all in. I laid down my hand and began reaching for the mound of money in the pot. That's when one of the players threw down four of a kind—fives. I watched him rake away his winnings.

I'd heard people say that America was a "land of opportunity." I wasn't exactly sure what that meant, but no matter how great the country, I knew I needed money to survive. I panicked. After everyone finished playing cards I pulled the man who had beaten me to the side and swallowed my pride. "You beat me fair," I said. "But I have to ask you to loan me ten dollars. I don't have any money left. I promise I will repay you when we get to America."

"How?" he said with a thin smile on his face. "How would you even find me to repay me?"

"I will find you. I always keep my word," I said. "I just can't get off this boat without any money. I'm not asking you to give me the money. Just a loan. That's all. Please. I wouldn't ask if I didn't need it." The man paused and thought for a moment. "I will repay you with interest," I pleaded. He reached into his pocket and pulled out the wad of dollars.

"Interest is not necessary. Just pay me the ten dollars," he said. He riffled off ten dollars and handed it to me.

"Thank you. I appreciate your kindness. I won't forget," I said.

I returned to my cabin, but my excitement that night made sleep difficult. My imagination raced with scenes of what America might look like. I felt a sense of pride that I was coming to the nation that freed me. I thought of the American soldiers I'd seen on liberation day at Buchenwald. Many were young, only a few years older than I was now. They had left their mothers and fathers, girlfriends and wives, to travel around the world to fight and die for me and others they did not know. Thinking about them brought tears of gratitude to my eyes. Any nation that could produce such men must be great, I figured.

Saturday, September 18, 1947. Smiles were everywhere. By late afternoon, I found a comfortable spot on the deck with a clear view of the ocean. I sat and looked for land over the water's edge and saw nothing. Night fell and the rain came. I moved under cover but stayed outside. I didn't want to miss seeing my new homeland. I peered through the sheets of rain and tried to focus my eyes. An hour into my watch, voices startled me.

"Look!" they said. "There!" A glint of light twinkled on the dark horizon. Then another, and another. A row of lights that sparkled like an impossibly long string of perfect diamonds strung across the dark sea.

News of the sighting spread quickly. Passengers bustled out onto the deck and lined the metal railings. The lights stretched higher, the luminous New York skyline growing bigger and brighter by the minute. I smiled and cried.

The boat slowed as we entered New York Harbor. An enormous, glowing statue beamed beautiful against the wet black sky. I had no idea what she meant, how she got there, or why.

I gazed at the shining cityscape. The buildings ran up and down in jagged peaks that stretched for miles. My eyes bounced from lighted block to lighted block—finally falling off into inky darkness at its outermost edges.

I was struck by the arresting feeling that my life was born anew, that a land capable of building something so splendid was capable of helping someone so small.

The *Ernie Pyle* docked. I couldn't wait to disembark. Since I had to go through immigration processing, I spent an impatient night on board. I had no desire to go inside my cabin. Instead, I would stay up all night watching over my new nation like a proud father watching his newborn sleeping. But I told myself I should try to get some rest so I'd be fresh to meet my family on my first big day in America.

The next morning, when I stepped off the ship, an immigration official and a Yiddish–English interpreter helped issue me a green card. "You are an American, but not a citizen," the official said.

"You are wrong. I am Czech," I said.

"No, no more. Now you're an American," he said.

"No, see, I was born in Pavlovo, Czechoslovakia," I said.

"I understand. But now you are an American. You aren't a citizen. Yet. From now on you have every right that I have except you have to report every year. If you obey the laws, you will be treated just like me," he said. "If in five years you decide you want to become a U.S. citizen and you take the required tests, you can officially become an American citizen. Okay?"

"Okay," I said.

I couldn't believe it. How could he say that to me? I'm an American? I just got here. I felt so grateful, so lucky, so undeserving. To me those were the biggest words I had ever heard. I took advantage of those words. *What a country,* I thought. *This really is the place to be.*

The official handed me my green card. I looked at it proudly. "I'm really an American?" I asked the interpreter.

"Yes," he said with a warm smile.

"Okay then," I said. "I'm an American!"

I didn't know what to do next. Uncle Irving had sent me a picture, but I didn't see anyone who looked like the man in the photograph. I looked all around for my friend Kalvin as well, but

I didn't see him either. Just as I started to feel a little uneasy, an old woman walked up to me. "Maximilian?" she asked in Yiddish.

"Yes, I'm Maximilian Grünfeld," I said. She flung her arms wildly around me, pelting me with kisses on my cheeks. I had no idea who she was.

"I'm your Aunt Elka, your mother's oldest sister!" she said. "Here, look." She held up an old picture of me taken well before we were rounded up and arrested. "Your Uncle Irving, my brother, sent me this picture of you and asked me to pick you up. You'll stay with me in the Bronx for a week before he comes to take you to Baltimore," she said.

"Oh, I see," I said, having no idea what she really meant. "So nice to... You see... The lights in the harbor on the...."

Aunt Elka stood and looked at me with big, brown eyes. I was her nephew, and even though she'd never seen me before, she loved me as part of her family.

"Thank you," I managed finally. "I'm so grateful you came."

"You look too skinny," she said, giving me a playful poke in the ribs. "We're going to fatten you up. I want you to meet my son-in-law, Joe." We shook hands and hugged. A few minutes later, I heard a familiar voice calling my name. It was Kalvin. He'd come just as he promised. I hugged him and introduced him to Aunt Elka and Joe Wernick. They offered Kalvin a ride with us.

The three of us walked in the rain to Joe's car, an impressive black, shiny Nash. I nudged Kalvin. "Reminds me of my big black Mercedes!" I said laughing.

"I remember that story," he said with a sly smile.

We drove through the streets of New York, the colors and shapes of the city a kaleidoscopic blur through the raindrops on the passenger window. Cars honked, lights flashed, and people tromped down slick sidewalks. The sight of stores everywhere made me happy. "So many stores," I said. "Does everyone have a job here?"

"Everyone who wants a job does," replied Aunt Elka.

We headed to Aunt Elka's small brownstone in the Bronx. We were greeted at the door by her Hungarian husband, Uncle Louie. We hugged, laughed, spoke Yiddish, and ate. "Well, what do you think of America so far?" Joe asked me.

"I love it!" I said. "I'm an American living in the Bronx of the New York!"

The family—*my* family—burst out in laughter.

"It's just 'the Bronx,'" said Joe. "We just say, 'the Bronx.'"

"Okay," I said. "I'm an American living in the Bronx!"

"Perfect," he said. "Just right."

That evening, the city's thousand sounds lulled me into the deepest sleep I'd experienced in years.

The next morning, Joe and Aunt Elka took me on a driving tour of the city. We had driven less than half a mile from their home when I saw a disturbing sight. An endless line of tired, miserable-looking people snaked around a massive, wide building. "I had no idea," I said in a concerned tone. "Things must be terrible here. These people are hungry? I've never seen so many people waiting in a breadline!"

"Sweetheart, that's not a breadline," said Aunt Elka. "That's Yankee Stadium!"

CHAPTER SEVEN

GGG

New York 1947. The city that year was magical.

The streets hummed with people and possibility. I arrived eleven days before the start of the legendary 1947 all–New York World Series. The Yankees' Joe DiMaggio, Yogi Berra, and Phil Rizzuto were set to take on Jackie Robinson, Pee Wee Reese, and Duke Snider of the Brooklyn Dodgers. It was Yankee Stadium in the Bronx versus Ebbets Field in Brooklyn. I knew nothing of baseball. What was unmistakable, however, was that the city was in full celebration.

I was, too. My aspirations were at an all-time high. I was young, strong, and eager. I had already fallen in love with New York during those first few days staying with Aunt Elka. Even though I was headed to Baltimore, something in me told me I'd find my way home to New York.

My cousin Mark Fendrich showed me the town and did his best to explain America to me. Mark was successful and handsome, with a face that reminded me of my mother's. He told me I had another maternal aunt, named Gussie, who also lived in Baltimore. Mark said the plans that had me moving to Baltimore to live with Uncle Irving had changed.

"You'll still be in Baltimore, but you'll be living with your first cousin, Frances Berman, and her husband, Moe," Mark explained. "Great people, very successful. Moe made his money in real estate and bail bonds. Frances is a milliner—makes the most gorgeous hats you've ever seen. They have a big, beautiful three-story home with plenty of extra room for you. They have three daughters, Barbara, Natalie, and Rikki. You'll love them. They can't wait to meet you. Cousin Frances is going to pick you up and drive you to her and Moe's home in Baltimore."

I hated to burden family, but I was grateful to have people that cared so much for me.

The Bermans' home on Callaway Avenue was just as promised. It was a huge white house with green shutters and six bedrooms. When Frances and I pulled up, the whole family came out to hug and greet me. Moe spoke Yiddish. The others spoke English. I walked into their immaculate home, and within minutes Frances and the three girls were sliding plates of delicious home-cooked treats in front of me.

The Bermans treated me like a king. It was like living in a luxury hotel, complete with maids and fine furniture. Every meal was a formal dining experience. The Bermans took me all around

Baltimore and made several introductions to people with whom I had no way of communicating. It was sweet. And awkward. The youngest child, Rikki, was about ten years younger than I, and I became the brother she had always wanted. I did my best not to disappoint her. We'd play little games while I tried to entertain her through silly facial expressions and hand gestures. Unless Moe was around to translate, though, we had no clear way to communicate.

After my first few nights in the house, Frances said the family wanted to buy me a nice suit for job interviews. She took me to the store and bought my first GGG suit. Named after the three Goldman brothers—William P., Mannie, and Morris—GGG was the premier manufacturer of hand-tailored men's suits in New York. I had already heard of GGG because my friend Kalvin worked there in the factory. Frances said a GGG suit was the best money could buy. I felt bad the family spent so much money on me. Until, that is, I put the suit on. It draped my body beautifully. I looked smart and sharp. If I couldn't speak English, at least the suit would speak for me.

"You look like an American," Frances said. "You've got a great American suit. Now all you need is a great American job. I think I know just the man and place."

Frances said Moe had spoken to a Mr. Ben Miller about hiring me to work for his furniture upholstery business. Best of all, Mr. Miller spoke Yiddish. Two days later, Mr. Miller pulled up to the Bermans' home in a big fancy Cadillac. He stepped out of the car wearing a dapper suit and walked slowly to the door with the help of a cane. That a rich and important man who had to walk with a cane took the time to drive himself to meet a nineteen-year-old refugee told me all I needed to know about Mr. Miller's character. When he offered me a job nailing upholstery, I took it.

That night I called Kalvin and shared the good news. He congratulated me on my new position but lobbied me to leave Baltimore and move to New York to work with him at GGG. He said we could be roommates and split the rent. I told him I would think about it but I wanted first to try my hand at the upholstery business. Mr. Miller had been so generous and kind. I didn't want to appear ungrateful or rude.

For the next three weeks, I worked in Mr. Miller's big upholstery factory wrapping and nailing fabric. I worked hard and did well. Mr. Miller liked my attention to detail. He said I worked harder than any employee he had ever hired. His compliments strengthened my confidence.

After work and dinner, Frances, Moe, and I would sit around the dining table and chat. I started to notice the delicate but unmistakable manner in which people who knew I was a survivor tried to steer the conversation toward the Shoah to see if I was willing to discuss my experiences. I understood their curiosity, but I found it hard to talk about what we went through. It wasn't just the emotional pain of dredging up all the death and darkness that made me reticent. I didn't think anyone would believe me. If I had grown up in America and someone told me the story, I'm not sure I would have believed it myself. Something that bleak, that grim seems impossible to survive. For it to have happened in a "civilized" society was inconceivable to most Americans.

Perhaps for that reason, I contemplated changing my name from Maximilian Grünfeld to something more American. One evening after dinner I asked Moe what he thought about the idea. "Yes, Maximilian Grünfeld might be tricky for some people to spell. It also sounds very ethnic," he said. "But Max Grünfeld isn't all that bad."

"Yes, but it doesn't sound American. I want a good, strong American name," I said.

Frances walked in from tidying up the kitchen and joined us at the dining table. She asked Moe to interpret and explain what we were discussing. "I love your name, Maxi. Why would you want to change it?" she asked.

"I'm an American now," I said. "I want a name that shows it."

I couldn't even speak English fluently and yet somehow I was convinced an all-American name change was in order. I had no way of knowing that our conversation would determine the branding of my future fashion business.

"Well," said Frances, "what kind of name are you thinking about?"

"Something similar to my real name, but different," I said.

"Similar but different," she said, her eyes wandering up to the ceiling. "Hmmm...."

"I want a name people will respect," I said.

Moe and Frances tossed out different names. Finally Frances blurted out, "What about Martin? Not Martin Grünfeld—Martin Greenfield?"

"I love that!" I said, smacking the table with my hand. "Moe, what do you think? Martin Greenfield?"

"Sounds good to me," he said. "Why not?"

Just like that, I became Martin Greenfield. That was the great thing about starting over in America—you got a fresh start.

Whatever you told people, you became. For example, when Kalvin got to America, he decided to make himself two years older. Even though Kalvin was actually younger than I, on paper he was older. He never tired of teasing me about that. "Listen, *young* man...," he would joke in an authoritative tone.

Maybe my business would have grown faster with an unusual brand name like Maximilian—who knows? Then again, Martin Greenfield possessed a certain dignity and heft. Better still, it was easy to say and spell. It worked.

As the weeks went by, my inability to communicate with the Berman girls and others frustrated me. As a kid in Pavlovo, I dreamed that one day I would become a doctor and help save people's lives. But here I was, nineteen years old, and I couldn't so much as write or understand a simple English sentence. I had no way of expressing myself to others, sharing my thoughts and feelings with them. It was uncomfortable, embarrassing. Every few days or so, when I spoke to Kalvin on the phone, I realized how fast and fluid our conversations were by contrast. And of course Kalvin wasn't making things any easier on me. "You should see the girls here in Brooklyn. If you were here, we'd be going out every night and setting the city on fire," he said. "You can take a train from Baltimore to Brooklyn and be here tonight. I've already talked to my supervisor. You have a GGG job waiting for you. You're great with your hands. Besides, you don't need any skills to start as a floor boy."

"I like the job I have right now just fine," I said. "It's the language that's the problem. I know I can learn English very fast. I know Czech, Hungarian, German, and Yiddish. I'm a quick learner and good with languages. I just have to make the time to take the English classes and study hard. The problem is I can't attend classes when I'm working."

"That's what I'm telling you! I took the classes here. You can too. They even have night classes so you can work in the day and learn English at night," he said.

"They do? At nighttime?" I asked.

"Yes!" he said.

"I'll think about it."

"You always say that, Max."

"It's Martin now! Martin Greenfield!"

"Okay, Martin Greenfield. Talk to you later."

If I was going to move to New York, I had to do it my way. I refused to show disrespect or ingratitude to the Bermans or Mr. Miller, so I needed to talk to them before making any decisions. The next day at work I spoke to Mr. Miller.

"Sir, I've been thinking about my job," I said. "You have been so good and kind to me. I am extremely grateful to you and always will be. But you see, I have this friend, he lives in Brooklyn now, and he said he can get me a job at GGG as a floor boy. He says New York is the place for a young man to be and that we can share an apartment together."

"I see," said Mr. Miller, tapping his pen on his desk. "Well, it sounds like an exciting opportunity. What's the problem?"

"Well, sir, I just don't want to hurt the Bermans. They, like you, have been so good to me. They opened their home when I first arrived, even though they had never met me. I just don't...."

"You don't want to hurt their feelings," he said.

"Exactly," I said. "It's just very hard for me to communicate with the kids. I'm not comfortable unless I do it on my own, without having to rely on someone to translate. I know I will learn English rapidly. They even have classes in Brooklyn where I can learn at night so I can work in the day. I just don't know how to tell the Bermans. I don't want them to think I'm ungrateful or disrespectful."

"Of course I'll help you," said Mr. Miller. "I will come to the house and be your interpreter for you. When they see that I'm there to support you, they will understand."

Mr. Miller came to the Bermans' home, just as he promised.

"Martin has asked me to come here to translate some very important things he wants to say to you," Mr. Miller said.

I explained that I loved each of them very, very much, that my heart was full of gratitude for how they had opened their home to me. I expressed how "thank you" could not begin to capture the depth of my appreciation for all they had done for me. However, I needed to learn the language, I explained. I didn't want to be a burden on them and had decided to get a train ticket to Brooklyn. I would work at GGG and live with my boyhood friend Kalvin.

"By Hanukkah," I said, "I will be speaking to you in English. You watch and see!"

Having Mr. Miller there to translate made all the difference. The Bermans were a loving lot. They understood and supported my decision. They said if ever I wanted to return to Baltimore, their home was my home.

The next week I took the train to Brooklyn.

⟳

I stepped off the train and saw a smiling Kalvin Mermelstein. "Welcome home to New York!" he said with his arms stretched wide. I gave him a big hug, and we headed for a small rental home on Thirteenth Street in Brooklyn. We rented one of the house's three tiny bedrooms. There was one small bed to share, a community bathroom, and a monthly rent of $6.50 each. It was perfect.

My first goal was to master English. Learning the language was, for me, a matter of respect. I lived here now; I was an American; I needed to speak English. In my experience, the best way to pick up a new language was to plunge right in. Shortly after arriving in Brooklyn, I signed up for night classes at Erasmus High School. My teacher there was a wonderfully patient and compassionate woman who used American traditions and customs as linguistic examples to excite our minds and encourage our studies. Few American customs piqued my curiosity more than baseball.

I wanted to understand baseball from the minute I saw that massive line of fans outside Yankee Stadium hoping against hope to get World Series tickets. Any sport that could make that many people stand for hours to buy a ticket must be spectacular, I figured. One of our early homework assignments was to bring a picture of something in America we wanted to learn more about. People brought pictures of movie stars, historical figures, and U.S. landmarks. I brought a baseball picture.

"You're interested in a sport called baseball," she said. "The best way for you to understand baseball is to see where it's played." She took a small scrap of paper and jotted something on it and handed it to me. "That's the address for Ebbets Field," she said. "That's where the Brooklyn Dodgers play baseball."

That weekend I found my way to Ebbets. No one was there. *If there's no game today, maybe I can at least see the playing field,* I thought. I walked around the massive building and jangled every gate, but they were all locked.

I approached my teacher after the next class. "I went to the address you gave me. It's locked up. I couldn't get in. Why would they lock up baseball?" I asked.

"Oh, no, you see, it's not baseball season right now!" she explained. "You have to wait until they begin playing games again during baseball season."

I didn't understand what she meant. In Pavlovo we played soccer whenever we wanted. Why we had to wait for the weather to change to see baseball I wasn't sure. But I could hardly wait.

Meanwhile, I was less excited about my work situation. Kalvin came through and got me a job at GGG making thirty-five dollars a week. I had no tailoring experience, so they started me as a floor boy running items around the wood plank floors. Hundreds of employees at dozens of stations worked inside the factory, which had opened in 1917. The whole operation confused the hell out of me. Had it not been for the racks of finished suits, I would have never been able to guess what product we were manufacturing.

The only experience I'd had with the tailoring of a suit was with the man in Prague who made my two suits. He was one person, and he made all the parts of the suit. But GGG was a massive operation with hundreds of workers creating suits in a piece-by-piece assembly line. The complexity confounded me. The initial language barrier didn't help either. Worse, there was one particularly nasty worker who, for whatever reason, enjoyed confusing me by refusing to speak Yiddish, even though he knew how.

By the end of my first week, I was ready to quit. I marched up to the GGG manager, Adolph Rosenberg. "I'm not sure this job is for me," I told him.

"You're doing fine. What's the problem?" he asked.

The Grünfeld family in Pavlovo, Czechoslovakia, 1934 or 1935. Left to right: Rivka (sister), Tzyvia (mother), Max (Martin), Joseph (father), and Simcha (another sister). Martin's younger brother, Sruel Baer, would be born later.

Allied Expeditionary Force Displaced Person ("AEF DP") registration card issued to Max Grünfeld, October 1946.

Photo from Martin's
Czech army ID.

Post-war index card listing Max
Grünfeld among prisoners arriving
at Buchenwald February 5, 1945,
and placed in Block 58, having left
Auschwitz January 27, 1945.

Date 2.5.50/PD	Bu/No.122816	GCC2/181/
Name GRÜNFELD, Maxmilian	File	-IB/9-
BD BP	Nat	
Next of Kin		
Source of Information	Buchenwald,Nachtrag zur Verände- rungsmeldung v. 27.1.45 Neu-	
Last known Location	zugänge v. Auschw.	Dated 5.2.45
CC/Prison Buchenwald	Bl. 22 lib.	
Transf. on	to	
Died on	in	
Cause of death		
Buried on	in	
Grave		D.C.No.
Remarks Page No. 21		

Bremerhaven

AMERICAN JOINT DISTRIBUTION COMMITTEE
LOCATION SERVICE BELSEN - CAMP

Date 12.2.48

Surname: Grünfeld   First Name: Max

Previous Name: Birthdate: age 19

Birthplace: Nationality: Czechosl.

Present Address: 529 W.Lexington St. Baltimore.Md.   Address before Deport:

Name of Father: Name of Mother:

Information Learned about above person:
Left Bremen for USA on SS Ernie Pyle on 11.9.47
by Joint

Information about Max Grünfeld filed with
the American Joint Distribution Committee
at Bergen Belsen DP camp, indicating that he
had sailed for the United States.

ABOVE: Peter Lundberg (left), Martin Greenfield (center), and Tod Greenfield (right) at Theresienstadt concentration camp, 1989.

RIGHT: Fake prisoners' bathroom at Theresienstadt built for Red Cross visit (top) and the actual bathroom (bottom). (Photos by Tod Greenfield)

Martin (center) at DP camp shortly before his departure for America.

Martin inside prison barracks at Theresienstadt, 1989.

Martin and his sisters, c. June 1936.

Martin rides a bicycle through the streets of Pavlovo, c. June 1936.

Martin in the meadow behind his childhood home in Pavlovo, c. 1989.

Martin's childhood home in Pavlovo, c. June 1936.

Entering Pavlovo from Mukačevo, 1989.

TOP: The man who built this log cabin in Pavlovo was a Christian who voluntarily maintained the Jewish cemetery for fifty years after the Jews of the town were taken away and murdered.

MIDDLE: On the street in Pavlovo, 1989.

BELOW: Martin outside his childhood synagogue in Pavlovo, 1989.

ABOVE: Visit to Pavlovo, 1989. The man in the white shirt is Shama Gelb, a cousin of Martin's who lived in Mukačevo. The man in the suit is the travel agent who arranged the trip. The boy is Shama's grandson. Tod's hand indicates where Martin carved his initials on the tree fifty years earlier.

RIGHT: A cold storage unit in Pavlovo (1989) like the one Martin's family used before the war. A stairway inside leads to a cold underground room.

◄ Martin today, photographed by Daniel D'Ottavio.

ABOVE: Martin and Arlene on their wedding day, December 23, 1956.

BELOW: David Greenfield's Bar Mitzvah, Temple Judea, Roslyn, NY, February 2006. Front: Bonnie, Amy, Rachel, Sophia, David, Arlene. Back: Tod, Jay, Cheryl, Martin.

LEFT: Jay Greenfield in the Red
Room at the White House,
February 2014, before one of
six appointments with President
Obama.

BELOW: Martin, President Obama,
Tod, and Jay in the president's
office in the White House.

RIGHT: With President Clinton during a fitting in his White House bedroom. Photo by George Stephanopoulos.

BELOW: Donna Karan and Martin Greenfield.

Tuxedo jacket made for LeBron James for the NBA All Star Party, February 2014.

Jay doing the first fitting with Leonardo DiCaprio for *The Wolf of Wall Street* in New York.

Jay admiring a new suit for Jonah Hill in his dressing room at NBC studios prior to Jonah's appearance on *Saturday Night Live*. Jonah wore the suit to the premiere of his movie *21 Jump Street* in March 2012.

ABOVE: Writer Wynton Hall, Martin Greenfield, and Steve Buscemi on the set of *Boardwalk Empire* in New York City (photo by Macall Polay, courtesy of HBO).

RIGHT: After the filming of episode seven of *The Blacklist* at Martin Greenfield Clothiers, Joseph Genuardi and Martin do a fitting for Red Reddington (James Spader).

Carmelo Anthony, with his wife, at the Metropolitan Ball in the navy rag & bone–style tails that Martin made for him.

Baz Luhrmann, with Catherine Martin, at the Metropolitan Ball in his Martin Greenfield tails.

Rag & bone's Marcus Wainwright and David Neville with their wives at the Metropolitan Ball in their tails by Martin Greenfield.

"This whole thing is stupid to me. I don't understand what I'm doing and how it makes a suit," I said. He chuckled. "I need this job and I'm grateful for it. But I cannot work unless something makes sense to me. I have to understand what I'm doing. Because when I do, I will do it better than anyone else."

Adolph Rosenberg understood me. He realized I had to understand the entire suit-making process to perform at my peak capacity. He was one of the best managers I've ever worked with. His brother, Sam, also worked at GGG and was in charge of pressing. The Rosenbergs were American born but also spoke Yiddish and Hungarian in addition to English. Were it not for Adolph Rosenberg's managerial instincts and patience, I might have exited the suit business altogether. He took me from station to station and explained the 108 operations that went into every GGG suit. Each worker specialized in making just one section of a suit, so he became an expert at it. The system also ensured consistency. The GGG manufacturing process was a breakthrough in the hand-tailoring industry. By the time Mr. Rosenberg was finished, I understood how all the pieces fit together to make something beautiful.

If the Nazis taught me anything, it was that a laborer with indispensable skills is less likely to be discarded. I was determined to learn every single task at GGG. I wanted to be the best, to stand out. Hand basting, darting, piping, facing and lining, blind stitching, pressing, armhole work, joker tags, fell stitching, preparing besoms, finishing—I would learn how to execute every procedure better than the person who taught me.

I also learned the importance of strong and open communication. You can learn from people at all levels. I have a grade-school education. Yet for decades I've made the finest men's suits in the world. I didn't need an expensive education. I watched, listened, asked questions, remained teachable, and devised ways to beat the best. I never aimed for mere excellence. Perfection was always my passion. Who wants to be second best? What's the point? If I was going to invest years learning the painstaking craft of hand tailoring, I would not stop practicing until I could make garments that danced.

No person at GGG was a better tailor than the firm's designer, Frank Perchacio. Barely over five feet tall, Frank was one of the best designers and tailors I've ever met, a legend. He'd been trained in Italy at a time when a tailoring apprenticeship could run seven or eight years. But Frank had also gone to design school in Chicago. His dual background gave him the rare ability both to dream up a design and to make it a reality through fine hand-crafted tailoring. He loved to innovate. In fact, Frank made the first "extra short" jacket that became a big seller with shorter customers.

Still, not all my interactions with GGG workers were as cordial and beneficial as those with Rosenberg and Perchacio. Ironically, it was my American Jewish colleagues I differed with most. We read from the same Torah and attended *schul* (synagogue) but had vastly different experiences. Many of them were Socialists or Communists, and I couldn't believe their ignorant embrace of failed ideologies. "You were born here," I told them. "You've never had the Russian Communists come in and seize everything. I have. Communism is not what you say it is. It is theft and murder. It's a lie. You don't know what you're talking about! How do you believe these ideas without investigating the reality?" I asked them.

Debate was futile. Their minds were made up. They stuck to their political theories without evidence or experience. I was sad, because many of them were sincere and hard workers. I decided it was best only to talk about suits, not society. There was no way for me to make them understand. They had been hoodwinked. I had seen the face of tyranny. They had not. They had the luxury of believing ideas whose consequences they never felt. I didn't.

Despite my differences with my colleagues and the annoyances they sparked, I could not have asked for a better place to hone my craft. Hand tailoring is a painstaking skill passed down from master tailors to apprentices over generations. At GGG, I stumbled into a treasure trove of knowledge and technical expertise. William P. Goldman, Frank Perchacio, Adolph Rosenberg—these men imparted wisdom and opportunities rare in the fashion industry. Looking back, my path to hand-tailoring perfection began that day at GGG when Mr. Rosenberg took me from station to station to learn the scores of steps that go into crafting world-class, flawless wares.

After a hard day of work at the GGG factory, Kalvin and I would hit the town at night after my English class. Nightclubs, Danny's Hideaway on Forty-Fifth Street, Thursday night dinners at the Doral Hotel, movies, double dates—we were living a young man's dream. We did it all.

After nearly three months in New York, I wanted to experience Washington, DC, for the first time. "If I don't see Washington, then I'm not an American," I said.

"Great. We'll go in the week between Christmas and New Year's," Kalvin said.

We took the train to Washington and stayed with one of Kalvin's aunts. Her husband was born in Pavlovo on the same day as my father, and the two became great friends. He owned a supermarket and had two daughters. It quickly became apparent that the family was trying to fix me up with the eldest daughter, who was in college. Her father suggested that she accompany Kalvin and me on our capital tour to help us navigate the city and assist with any English translation needs we may encounter.

My love affair with America only deepened. The Capitol, the White House—I never dreamed that decades later I would make suits for the men inside those buildings. All I knew was that there was nothing I did not love about my nation's capital. Kalvin and I wanted to see and experience everything. We toured the museums with free admission. When I arrived in America, I was told that in five years I could take a test on American history and become a citizen. I had to study Washington. President Abraham Lincoln and the Constitution joined General Dwight Eisenhower as my favorite symbols of America. Like Eisenhower, Lincoln had freed the slaves. When we went to the Lincoln Memorial and stood before that austere marble statue, I smiled. The men who put this country together made me proud. The Constitution—the radical idea that people should control the government, not the other way around—astounded me. I loved it all the more because I knew how revolutionary and rare an idea that truly was.

Unrepentant tourists, we made our way over to the U.S. Senate. With our host's daughter at the ready to translate, we struck up conversations with anyone who looked like he would talk to us.

An older, important-looking man walked up to us and asked if we were enjoying our time in the nation's capital.

"It's incredible. I never dreamed it would be this beautiful," I said in broken English.

"Where are you visiting from?" he asked.

"Brooklyn, New York," I said.

"Our neighbors to the north," he said. "That's wonderful."

"My name is Martin Greenfield. This is my friend Kalvin Mermelstein," I said.

"Nice to meet you. I'm Alben Barkley. I'm a United States senator from Kentucky," he said.

"A senator?! Such an honor to meet you, sir," I said.

"Yes, such an honor to meet you," said Kalvin.

"The honor is all mine," he said. "Where are you from originally?"

"We come from Pavlovo, Czechoslovakia," I said. "We came to America after the liberation." Senator Barkley paused and stepped closer.

"Were you in the concentration camps?" he asked in a hushed tone.

"Yes, sir."

"Where?" he asked.

"Auschwitz and Buchenwald," I said. Senator Barkley looked stunned.

"Do you have time for lunch today?" he asked. "It would be my privilege to take you to lunch. After we won the war I went to Germany and toured the camps myself. Saw the bodies. Saw it all. It was horrific, the most horrible thing I've seen in all my life. I would be most interested in hearing about your experiences."

Kalvin and I shot wide-eyed glances at each other. "Yes, sir!" we said at the same time.

While we sat and ate, Barkley peppered us with questions. Anything we didn't understand, our female friend translated. He wanted to know everything. I was struck by how knowledgeable he was about Hitler, the Nazis, and the concentration camps. As it turned out, Barkley had visited Buchenwald on April 24, 1945, when I was still there. Here is how Barkley remembered the experience in his 1954 memoir, *That Reminds Me*:

> Another experience, the horror of which shall be engraved on my memory as long as I live, was my trip to Germany early in 1945 as chairman of a joint Congressional committee to inspect Nazi extermination centers. As the American Army began to drive into Germany, General Eisenhower, then the Allied commander, recommended to General Marshall, Chief of Staff in Washington, that Congress be asked to send a committee to view these camps, because they were so atrocious and horrible that it was hard to believe, without seeing them, that such things existed.... We visited Buchenwald, Nordhausen and Dachau, names that will remain forever infamous. What we saw was loathsome beyond description: looking at the starved, dead bodies, piled in courtyards like cordwood, even hung on hooks like cattle in a slaughterhouse, made one want to reach out and seize a club or a gun and start punishing the guilty parties.

He was genuinely and deeply interested in us and the hell I endured. That a man of his power and prominence would take time out of his schedule to treat two poor refugee boys to lunch astounded me.

"I want to stay in touch with you boys if that's okay," he said.

"That would be wonderful, sir," said Kalvin.

"I would like that very much, sir," I said.

"Here now, write down your mailing address so I have your information," he said.

I thought for sure he was just being polite. I never expected he would write. But he did. More than once.

A year later, Alben William Barkley became the thirty-fifth vice president of the United States.

Spring in Brooklyn. Baseball season finally rolled around, and I couldn't wait to see my first game. Tickets in the nosebleed seats were a quarter, and I made my first trip to Ebbets Field by myself. The crowd, the cheering, the spectacle—I was hooked. The players spit, spun, swung. I had no idea which team won or lost. But being in the stadium, shoulder to shoulder with all the citizens, made me feel like a true American. I felt like I belonged.

After English class, I told my teacher about my first baseball game. I loved the experience, I told her, but was more confused about the rules of the game than before I went. "If I buy your ticket to the game, will you go with me and explain the rules?" I asked shyly. She agreed, and off we went.

Ebbets Field proved to be the ultimate American classroom. My teacher turned the baseball diamond into a chalkboard. She made me pronounce every position, every rule. She taught me about runs, innings, and strikes. She made me read the signs and billboards. She quizzed me to make sure I understood the rules. When I'd get an answer wrong, she'd giggle and gently correct me.

Around the eighth inning, I looked out across the lush green field and up into the clear blue sky. A soft breeze blew against my face. I was struck by the improbability of the moment. My life was a miracle. The crack of a baseball bat had replaced the smack and sting of a flogging stick. I had friends and family. I had a green card. I had a job and a chance. I had Jackie Robinson. A rush of gratitude overcame me—a feeling that my life had a meaning and purpose that I couldn't fathom, that by some astonishing act of divine benevolence I'd been one of the fortunate few who were spared the flames.

Back then, people called New York the Wonder City. It was. But that was only half right. America, my beloved new home, was the Wonder Country. I couldn't get enough. Within a couple of months, my teacher had given me the gift of English. Language was a currency I would not squander.

⁓

Money was tight. I decided to free up my food budget by taking a second job at night pressing clothes. It paid no money, but I was remunerated with a daily meal, and the invaluable knowledge I gained more than compensated for the lack of financial reward. Working as a presser brought me closer to clothes and was my introduction to fabrics. The quality of a suit—how it stands up against the needle, how it drapes, how it moves, how it withstands stains and the elements—begins with the fabric.

My eyes and fingers learned to distinguish quality fabrics from cheaper textiles. Without looking at the brand label, I'd examine a jacket's fabric—thumb the weave, inspect the buttonholes (buttonholes on quality suits are sewn by hand, not machine), and run my fingers down and across the lining. I'd guess whether the jacket in my hands was made by a well-known designer or was a cheap knockoff before opening the suit and reading the tag. By the end of two weeks, I never guessed wrong.

Yet as valuable as my short stint as a presser was, no one was more important in my education than the owner of GGG, Mr. William P. Goldman. One of five brothers and the mainstay of the business since he founded it at the age of thirty, Mr. Goldman taught me everything I know about the hand-tailored menswear business.

Mr. Goldman took an instant liking to me. To increase my efficiency, I'd had a carpenter build a large box in which I organized all my spools and materials at my station. Mr. Goldman and Adolph Rosenberg had been surveying stations, when my box caught Mr. Goldman's eye. "What is that?" he asked.

"Open it and show him," said Rosenberg.

Inside, all my spools, needles, tailor's tape, and other supplies were organized and at the ready. "I did it this way to avoid wasting time going back and forth to get materials," I explained.

"Brilliant," said Mr. Goldman. "Absolutely perfect." He loved anything that increased efficiency and reduced costs or waste. From that moment on, I was a standout in his mind. He always called me "Martino." One day I asked him why. He said, "Many of the best tailors are Italian. So I call you Martino because I think one day you're going to outshine even the Italians." When he was alive, I never called Mr. Goldman by his first name. I still don't. I respect him too much.

A tall, distinguished, grandfatherly looking man with a soft face, thin lips, and piercing eyes, Mr. Goldman always wore a GGG suit when circulating on the factory floor. After his rounds, he'd throw on his tailor's apron and head straight to the cutting room. He loved cutting because his father, who was also a tailor, had taught him the art. On Thursdays Mr. Goldman worked out of the company office on Fourteenth Street in Manhattan.

Mr. Goldman was from the old school. He treated his workers with respect, and his handshake meant something. At lunchtime he would handpick a half-dozen workers to eat with him. There was only one rule for these luncheons: you couldn't talk about work, only your family, hobbies, interests, or life. Mr. Goldman wanted to understand people, listen to them, validate their issues, and address their concerns. When a worker needed something, he tried to help him out. When an employee had a request, he instructed his managers to do their best to accommodate it.

After working at GGG a while, I'd saved up a few hundred bucks and decided to buy a jalopy and fix it up myself. One of the first things I'd noticed about Americans was their love affair with the automobile, and it had become my goal to own my own car. I couldn't afford a new car, or even a used one. I could, however, afford a broken-down 1937 Pontiac with a busted engine. So I bought it—$225 for the car and another $25 to tow it off the lot. Given my experience as an auto mechanic, I knew that, with time, I could rebuild the car's engine. The trouble was I had nowhere to park the thing. When Adolph Rosenberg heard about my dilemma, he said I could park the car behind the factory for free. Better still, he gave me permission to work on the car after hours. After several months, I successfully rebuilt the engine. I was among the first refugees to own a car.

The second "G" in GGG was Morris Goldman, the head of sales. It was a great job for him because he liked to take risks and go for the big payoff. That desire to beat the odds and score big fueled his passion for horse racing. In fact, Morris took me to my first horse race. He taught me how to bet and how to pick the best horses.

Mannie Goldman was the third "G." Someone once said that Mannie was the kind of man who wakes up in the morning wondering what he can do for someone. An elegant man with powerful connections to presidents, celebrities, and business barons, he traveled frequently and was in charge of fashion trends. When he wasn't globetrotting to gather new swatches and styles, Mannie came by the factory every afternoon around four o'clock to make sure operations ran smoothly.

The younger Goldman brother, Abe, came to work at GGG later. The most eccentric boss I ever had, Abe was mysophobic. His fear of germs was so severe that during GGG parties he stood near the bar to drink Scotch so he could be near alcohol to cleanse his hands. When we sewed the buttonholes on his suits, Abe made us douse the silk in alcohol so that the thread where his hands would touch when buttoning his jacket wouldn't be tainted. Ironically, Abe died from infection.

The Goldman brothers were a philanthropic clan, establishing the William P. Goldman & Brothers Foundation, which exists to this day. Mr. Goldman's generosity came in many different forms. After six months at GGG, I'd already worked my way up from floor boy to fitter to blind stitcher. One day Mr. Goldman walked over to my station to inspect my stitching. He held up a piece of my work and ran his fingers along my stitch line. "Quality work, Martino. Quality work," he said.

"Thank you, sir," I replied.

"Do you enjoy working here?"

"Yes, sir. Very much."

"So you want to be a tailor for life?"

"I'm not sure, sir," I answered. "When I was growing up I always thought I wanted to be a doctor. But I heard here in America it takes a long time and a lot of money to be a doctor."

"Do you know how long that will take? You'll be sixty years old before you become a doctor. I can give you the same money and promote you to an assistant supervisor. You'd then be an executive. I'll even put you on the profit-sharing plan and waive the five-year rule. Martino, I will make you a *suit* doctor!"

"A *suit* doctor!" I chuckled. "Wow, thank you, sir. That's very generous of you. I accept!"

"Happy to do it," he said. Mr. Goldman put his hand on my shoulder and stared intently at me. "Martino, have I ever told you the secret to success in this business?" he asked.

"No, sir," I said.

"Would you like me to?"

"Very much."

"Success in this business is about producing quality with intrinsic value." I nodded but didn't know what "intrinsic" meant. "What that means, Martino, is that a man will pay more for a GGG suit because he knows we use superior materials and production than our cheaper competitors," he explained.

"I see," I said.

"So even though we cost much more, they pay it, because they know our suits are the best in the industry and therefore last much, much longer," he said.

Produce quality with intrinsic value.

Mr. Goldman's words became my motto. Quality is the greatest bargain.

When Kalvin and I weren't working, we were fumbling our way through courtship and romance. Our GGG suits made us the best-dressed refugees in all of Brooklyn. But we had yet to master the art of approaching a young woman properly, face-to-face, wooing her with charm and wit.

Young women lived in our two-story rental house: two plump sisters who shared a bedroom and a striking model who hogged the community bathroom in the mornings, leaving Kalvin and me to vie for the shower to get ready for work. To avoid waiting in line during her hour-long beauty ritual, we were forced to wake up thirty minutes early.

One morning while getting ready for work, I walked to our window and looked out. My eyes slowly scanned the street before floating to the windows of the building directly across from ours. There, framed in an open window, stood a girl with silky blond hair and a sweet smile. I stood and watched as she talked to someone inside her house. The girl laughed and gestured frequently with her hands. Her vibrant energy captivated me. All of a sudden she turned toward the window and locked her eyes on mine, jolting me out of my stare. I quickly raised my hands and pretended to be closing the window. Yet even as I lowered the glass pane, I gazed at her. She didn't look away. In fact, she waved. I smiled wide and waved back.

For a week I made it a point to look for her on the street outside our house when walking to and from my jobs. Finally, I saw her entering her home.

"Hi there. I'm Martin," I said, extending my hand.

"Nice to meet you. I'm Helen. Helen Vitalis. How long have you lived here?" she asked. I didn't know if she meant the rental house or America.

"Oh, well, I've been roommates with my friend Kalvin for the last several months," I said. "We work together at GGG. We're tailors."

"Wow," she said, "that's great."

A dating relationship soon started.

Helen's father, who liked me from the beginning, was an announcer on the Greek radio station. Her mother was an attractive Ukrainian. On weekends Mr. Vitalis drove Helen and me in his big Ford to the beach, to dinner, or anywhere else we wanted to go.

Helen's older sister, Maria, was in her twenties and a semiprofessional singer. One night Helen invited me to go with her to Manhattan to hear Maria perform on the radio program *Your Hit Parade*. "I think you'll enjoy it," said Helen. "They hand out free packs of Lucky Strike cigarettes." I smoked Chesterfields but didn't have the heart to burst her bubble. Besides, free cigarettes were free cigarettes.

We arrived at the venue and, sure enough, attendants handed out free packs of Lucky Strikes. I grabbed several packs and stuffed them in my jacket pockets. As I'd learned train hopping in my black-market trading days, a committed smoker would trade items of value for a pack of his favorite smokes.

"This is so exciting to get to see your sister sing," I said. Maria walked on stage and took her place alongside the other two backup singers. She sang with confidence and poise. After the performance, Helen and I waited for Maria to come out and greet us. We congratulated her on her performance.

"Some of the singers and I are going to a restaurant a block away to blow off some steam. Would you like to join us?" she asked.

I didn't drink alcohol but was happy to go anyway. "That would be lovely," I said.

"Wait right here. I'll get the others so we can walk together," said Maria. She returned with the crooner and two backup singers. "Martin and Helen, please meet our leader, Frank Sinatra," said Maria.

"Thanks for coming," said Sinatra. "Hope you enjoyed the performances tonight."

"It was beautiful," I said. "You were spectacular. I loved it."

"Great," said Sinatra. "Let's go."

We walked down the street as a group to the restaurant to grab a bite. Sinatra wanted a drink.

I had heard Sinatra's name before but knew almost nothing about him. He had released only two albums to that point, *The Voice of Frank Sinatra* in 1946 and *Songs by Sinatra*. His voice was pure magic. But as a poor Holocaust survivor on a razor-thin budget, I was just as interested in the free packs of smokes as in meeting Sinatra for the first time.

I enjoyed spending time with Helen, but I wasn't sure she was the girl for me. Eager to get Mr. Goldman's assessment, I brought her to GGG for a New Year's dinner and introduced them. Later, I asked him what he thought. "Well, Martino, she's a beautiful woman," he told me. "But if you're asking me if she's the girl you should marry, I have to say no."

"Why? What makes you say that?" I asked.

"Well, I just think you should get a nice Jewish girl, that's all," he said.

CHAPTER EIGHT

THE BEAUTIFUL PEOPLE

During the summer of 1948, I realized Mr. Goldman was right: Helen wasn't the girl for me. It wasn't anything she did, but what I had yet to do: live, roam, explore. America is big—huge, in fact. There were encounters to be had, lessons to be learned. Put simply, I realized I was not ready for marriage. It was unfair to lead Helen on or waste her time. Still, I didn't know how to break it off. I didn't want to hurt her. She and her family had been nothing but kind. What's more, having lost everyone I ever loved, I was terrible with good-byes.

The solution to my cowardly breakup dilemma arrived in the form of a letter I received from my uncle in Mexico. Uncle Antonio Berger had no children. He lived most of his life in France but moved to Mexico when he was unable to gain entry into the United

States. Like my other maternal aunts and uncles, Uncle Antonio never met my mother, having left Pavlovo before her birth. Uncle Antonio and I had maintained regular correspondence from the time Uncle Irving included his mailing address in those early letters sent to Gabersee. In his latest letter, Uncle Antonio informed me he would be sending me an airplane ticket to Mexico to visit him. He said the ocean was clear, the girls were gorgeous, and the weather was perfect—a paradise for a much-needed getaway.

I had never ridden on an airplane. The idea of flying to a vacation destination was foreign to me. In my mind, civilian aviation was for rich, famous people, not common people. And certainly not broke refugees. The timing was perfect, though. The factory closed every summer for the union holiday.

That summer, when the sun baked Brooklyn like a brick, Uncle Antonio told me to keep an eye on the mail for his paid airline ticket and to prepare for a week of pure bliss in Mexico. Uncle Antonio had done well for himself in the real estate and jewelry businesses. His generosity moved me, but it was getting to spend time together and strengthen the family ties that excited me most.

Kalvin understood this and was happy for me. He was also glad that at least one of us would be able to say he had flown on an airplane. "Big shot! Maybe you'll meet movie stars or singers. You never know," he said, giving me a brotherly chuck on the shoulder.

My Mexico adventure gave me a way to let Helen down easy and go our separate ways. Instead of telling her I was going on a one-week vacation to Mexico, I told her I was *moving* to Mexico. Permanently. Since we lived next door to one another, my ruse forced Kalvin and me to move. Relocating was easy. Everything we owned fit into a couple of suitcases and boxes. Besides, we had wanted a larger place, and now we had an excuse—bad as it was—to find one.

I spent some money on a nice necklace, and when I put it around Helen's neck, I told her she could always look at it and think of the fun and memories we shared. "I'll always care for you," I said, meaning every word, "but you and I need our freedom to live and love. You're a wonderful, beautiful woman. Happiness will always find you."

Kalvin and I then decamped to the Hotel Brickman, a popular Jewish vacation spot in the Catskills. The resort offered a special summer rate for single young men and women, just thirty-five dollars for an entire week's lodging with swimming, tennis, ping-pong, and other activities. I figured I would stay several days and return in time to receive Uncle Antonio's airplane ticket.

Scores of young women and men came for the singles' special. The only objective was having fun. My life to that point had been one of constant work, so the notion of traveling for pleasure was entirely foreign to me. Our simple lives in the Carpathian Mountains never included luxury resort accommodations. *I could get used to this,* I thought. After three days of soaking up the sun and enjoying the company of the girls, I received word that Uncle Antonio had purchased a ticket on American Airlines and that my flight departed the next day. Kalvin, Aunt Elka, and her family came to the airport to see me off.

On my first flight from New York to Dallas, I felt like an aristocrat. I sat in a window seat. The plane buzzed down the runway and took flight, hovering over New York City. The aerial view of the massive metropolis was mesmerizing and sent my mind flashing back to my arrival in America less than a year before, when I stood on the deck of the *Ernie Pyle* staring at the Statue of Liberty. So much had changed. I now knew what she was and meant.

The plane lifted through the clouds and drifted dreamlike above them. I wondered what Mexico and my uncle would be like. Uncle Antonio's letters were warm and welcoming. Earlier that year, I'd mentioned in a letter I was still contemplating becoming a doctor. Uncle Antonio told me he would be happy to help me through college. I appreciated the gesture, but that wasn't my style. Whatever I received, I had to earn. Yet the generous offer to a nephew he had never met confirmed the goodness of his heart.

The plane made its descent into Dallas. The next leg of the trip required me to go through immigration to enter Mexico. The line was long and my flight full. When I got to the front, I showed the official my ticket and green card. His eyes hopped back and forth between my face, ticket, and green card. "Sir, I'm sorry, but we cannot let you into Mexico," he said quietly.

"Excuse me?" I said.

"It says here you were born in Czechoslovakia. Is that correct?"

"Yes. Pavlovo, Czechoslovakia."

"Yes, well, sir." He cleared his throat. "That is a Communist country. We cannot allow you to board the flight to Mexico."

"I know it's a Communist country. That's why I left Czechoslovakia and came to America! I'm very aware it's a Communist country."

"We can't allow you to fly, sir."

"You don't understand. My Uncle Antonio Berger lives in Mexico. He was the one who bought me the plane ticket. I have a green card. In a few more years I will be an American citizen. I just need to get to Mexico to see my uncle. He's waiting for me."

"Sir, I'm going to have to ask you to step aside so I can help the next customer. Maybe my supervisor can help you," he said dismissively.

I waited. The supervisor couldn't help me. They handed me off to the American immigration officials, who said they would send a limo to pick me up and take me to a nearby hotel until the situation was resolved.

"Driver, what hotel are we going to?" I asked.

"One of the nicest hotels in all of Dallas, sir," he said. "The Hotel Adolphus."

We pulled up to the massive brick hotel and the driver let me out. I stepped into splendor. Ornate moldings, sparkling crystal chandeliers, mahogany-paneled walls, a grand staircase—the Hotel Adolphus, which is still operating, was magnificent. *I could really get used to this,* I thought.

The hotel's Century Room featured entertainers and musical acts. At the check-in desk, I asked who would be performing that week. "Doris Day," said the front-desk attendant. Her tone suggested that Miss Day was someone of importance. I had no idea who she was but decided I would see her perform before leaving.

From my room, I called Uncle Antonio to explain the situation. He said he had several high-powered contacts and connections in Mexico. Whether those individuals extended to the consulate he wasn't sure, but he would do all he could to resolve the situation.

In the meantime, I figured if I had to be stuck in Dallas and have a room at the Adolphus on American Airlines' dime, I might as well make the best of it and experience the city. I flipped through the Yellow Pages and found a Jewish social club before calling for the driver. Checking my white suit in the mirror one last time, I went down to the car and hopped in like I owned it.

The driver drove me to the address I gave him. The sign out front said, "The Columbian Club." I opened the car door and began to step out.

"Sir," the driver said, "I'm pretty sure you have to be a member to get in."

"Don't worry about that," I said, before shutting the door.

The GGG suit I was wearing was top of the line. Better still, it was white. Most people my age owned only a navy-blue or charcoal-gray suit, if any. Wearing a white suit tailored to the nines was a symbol of wealth and distinction. It said, "This kid has money, or belongs to someone who does." If I projected a confident demeanor, I knew I could slip in.

Sure enough, the doorman gave me the once-over and welcomed me with a smile. "I'm a guest," I said while walking. "I'm meeting my party shortly." A hand-tailored suit and a steady demeanor. That's all it took to make things happen.

I went to the main dining room, ordered a meal, and signed the charges to American Airlines before striking up conversations with a few waitresses. They wanted to know who I was. I told them I was headed to Mexico on business. When they asked what line of work I was in, I simply told them "fashion." They were impressed.

I noticed a pretty young woman sitting by herself near a window. When I caught her eye, she smiled. I walked over to her. After about an hour of friendly conversation, I asked if she would join me for dinner. I had no money to take her out, but I did have my room and food covered at the Hotel Adolphus. "Tonight I'd like to take you somewhere special. Have you ever eaten at the Hotel Adolphus?" I asked her.

"No, never," she said.

"Well, tonight we'll fix that," I said in my most debonair tone.

"That would be lovely," she said excitedly.

In my mind I was a regular Casanova. I laid it on extra thick. "Do you like music?" I asked.

"Yes, of course," she said.

"Would you like to see Doris Day in concert with me tonight?" I asked with a sly smile.

"Doris Day! I love her! That would be wonderful!" she gushed.

That night we ate fine food at the Adolphus and were treated to the incredible Doris Day. I had seen enough American movies to know this was the kind of sweep-you-off-your-feet romance and spontaneity American women apparently loved. If nothing else, I figured this must be how it feels to be a business tycoon or Hollywood mogul—the kind of gent who could afford the Hotel Adolphus's pricey hotel rooms.

After a night like that, I was in no rush for the government officials and American Airlines to resolve my immigration situation. The next four days, I went to the Columbian, wooed girls, secured dinner dates, had "my" driver take me back to the hotel, showed off my "home away from home" at the Adolphus, and enjoyed fine dinners followed by another performance of the incomparable Doris Day.

After nearly a week in Dallas, American Airlines offered to fly me back to New York *gratis*. They had flown me to Dallas without informing me that my Czechoslovakian ancestry and non-U.S. citizen status would prevent me from entering Mexico and apologized for the inconvenience. That wasn't good enough. "I'm not going to fly with your airline. I want back the money my uncle paid you. Now!" I demanded. Tired of dealing with me, they coughed up the cash. I went to the railway station and asked how much it would cost to ride the train from Dallas to New York. The trip would take at least a day and a half and cost thirty-five dollars. I bought a ticket for the next train to New York.

The train was filled with U.S. soldiers. The parade of uniforms reminded me of mine. I envied those men on the train. I wanted to join the American Army when I got here. When I registered for the draft, they made me a 4-F because of my hand injuries. I begged the recruitment officer, insisting, falsely, that I was fine. (I later had to undergo extensive reconstructive hand surgery.) But it was to no avail.

Our train stopped in St. Louis, Missouri, for a layover. With a couple of hours to burn, I scanned the bustling waiting area for an open seat and sat down. A few minutes later, a towering white civilian walked up, grabbed me by the tie, and yanked me up and on my feet. I punched him. Two policemen raced over to untangle us. "He almost choked me, officer!" I said.

"You hit him! We saw you do it!" barked one of the policemen.

"He choked me! What would you have done? I don't even know this man! Why in the hell did he rush me and try to choke me with my necktie?!" I said.

"Sir," said the officer, "you were sitting in the colored section."

"I was *what?*" I asked.

"The colored section. You're white. These people are black," he said.

I looked around. He was right. To a person, the people in my section were black.

"You're not supposed to sit here," the officer explained. "See those drinking fountains? Look at the signs."

This was the first time in America I had been confronted with segregation. I didn't understand. Before I was liberated from Buchenwald, I had never seen a black person. Then, in another country somewhere, I saw a black soldier without a gun. I was told he wasn't allowed to carry a weapon, because of his skin color. Segregation struck me as ignorant and hateful. But that took place in a different country. I wasn't aware how deep the color line ran in America.

The year I arrived in America was the year Jackie Robinson desegregated baseball. It was also the first time a racially integrated team played in a World Series. But I'd never seen segregation in a public setting, not until I came to St. Louis. Indeed, many years later I learned that the famous entertainer Josephine Baker, a native of St. Louis, refused to perform in her hometown until 1952, when its segregation laws were eased.

I looked around the train station and saw no open seats. I sat back down in the black section. A few minutes later, the train was ready to go. So was I.

I got on the train and put my suitcase in the seat beside me. A flirty blond girl asked if I was saving the seat for someone. "No," I said, waving her into the seat. "Where are you headed?"

"The Poconos," she replied.

I didn't know what that meant, but she was pretty.

"Wonderful," I said. "I'm going to Brooklyn, New York."

We hit it off. Within a couple hours I had my arm around her and we kissed.

"You should come with me to the mountains!" she said. She was energetic, girlish, cute.

"Oh, I...I'm not sure. I need to be getting on to...."

"*Please?* Come on. It will be fun! I promise."

"Well...you see...the truth is I don't have enough money with me. I got stuck in Dallas for days and...."

"Don't worry about that. I have money. My family is rich. You're coming with me," she said, kissing my cheek.

At the next train stop I called Kalvin and asked him to wire me some money. He refused and asked why I wasn't in Mexico. When I told him I didn't have time to explain, he got annoyed and hung up. I hopped back on the train.

"I can't let you pay for me," I told the girl. "I tried to get my roommate to wire me money but he wouldn't."

"Why are you still talking about money? You're coming with me, remember? I already decided that."

I went to the Poconos.

We spent two fun-filled, romantic days at an enchanting resort in the Poconos. The carefree life of the upper class appealed to me. I never imagined people lived so spontaneously. I wanted to earn that kind of personal freedom for myself. I wanted to be somebody.

With exactly enough money to take the train to Grand Central and the subway to Brooklyn, I returned home and told Kalvin all about my new "girlfriend." She and I exchanged a few letters, but I never saw her again.

As for Helen, I only saw her once more. Kalvin and I went to a movie. I looked down in the front rows and there she was. I couldn't stand the thought of facing her, so I got up and left.

Traveling through America helped me discover who I was and what I wanted. It taught me not to settle for second best, either personally or professionally. I wasn't going to marry just anyone. I would wait for my dream girl. Same thing for my career. I was in it for the long run. I didn't want to work for a suit company; I wanted to *own* a suit company. I aspired to do things my way, earn the funds and freedom to travel on airplanes, enjoy luxurious vacations.

Those first two years in America confirmed that I had arrived in a nation of infinite possibilities. They gave me cause to dream. A life of mediocrity held no interest for me. I wanted to run and work with the best.

Five years to the day I arrived in America, I became a U.S. citizen. The patriotic pride I felt that day has never ebbed. It has intensified. There isn't a person who loves America more than I do. The United States is the best damn country the world has ever known. Anyone who questions that hasn't been where I've been, hasn't seen what I've seen.

∽

I maximized every opportunity GGG gave me. By 1956, I had worked my way up from supervisor to head quality man in charge of inspecting garments at all stages of production to ensure proper quality. The job paid $110 a week, enough to support the one thing I wanted most: a family of my own.

In April, a coworker's wife set me up on a blind date with a "gorgeous girl" a few months younger than I. She had graduated from Lincoln High School in Coney Island and worked as an executive secretary at Fuller Fabrics. "That's all I know. Here's her name and number," my coworker said, handing me a piece of paper. "Give her a call or don't." I read her name: "Arlene Bergen." Sounded like a good Jewish name. *What the heck?* I thought. *Give her a call. He did use the word "gorgeous," after all.*

I called Arlene. I could tell my strong accent threw her off. She seemed nice enough but said the soonest she could get together was in two weeks—on a Wednesday, no less. I didn't know if that was her polite way of blowing me off. I took my chances and set the date.

The day of our blind date, I washed and waxed my beige and black Mercury and pressed my GGG suit before making my way to her family's home in Sea Gate. Her parents greeted me at the door and ushered me into their living room to wait until Arlene emerged. A stunning, petite brunette with alluring blue eyes and a sweet smile walked into the living room and stopped time.

You know those moments in your life that you know—absolutely know to the core of your being—that something life altering, something momentous just happened? This was one of those moments.

What I did not know at the time was that three other young men—all of whose names began with "M"—were courting her as well. She had instructed her mother not to use my first name for fear she might slip up and accidently refer to me as Morty, Milton, or Morris.

Had I known how gorgeous she was—and how much competition I was up against—I might have planned a more romantic date. Instead, I took Arlene to a Brooklyn nightclub called Ben Maksik's Town and Country at Flatbush Avenue and Avenue V. The club was considered one of the area's hot spots, with people coming in from Manhattan to see and be seen. We danced all night.

A couple of dates later I asked Arlene to go steady with me. She refused. "I don't believe in 'going steady,'" she said confidently. "You either know what you want and are serious enough to marry me, or you don't."

What an answer, I thought. *What a woman.* From then on, I knew Arlene was the girl for me.

A few months later, I went shopping in the city for an engagement ring. After visits to several jewelry stores, my shopping came to an abrupt end when I walked into the next shop and discovered that the proprietor, incredibly enough, was the man I had borrowed ten dollars from on the *Ernie Pyle.* "Remember me?!" I said smiling.

"I'm...I'm afraid I...."

"The boat! The *Ernie Pyle.* The poker game!" I said.

"Oh...yes, yes, yes. I remember now. Yes," he said smiling.

"You loaned me the ten dollars. I promised I would repay you. I'm here to repay you by buying my girl's engagement ring from you!" I said.

We looked at ring after ring and shared all that had happened since arriving in America. He tried to extend an extra discount. I refused. A fair price was all I wanted; I was happy to see him make a profit. "Consider it an interest payment on the loan," I said with a chuckle.

Arlene and I were married December 23, 1956, when the GGG factory shut down for the Christmas holiday. Mr. Goldman prayed over the *challah* (bread) and cut it.

Shortly after the wedding, we rented a small apartment in Brooklyn on Ocean Parkway near Brighton Beach. The first week of marriage, Arlene and I brought home paychecks. Hers was $115. Mine was $110. The next day I took both checks to GGG and found Mr. Goldman. "Here's my wife's check. And here is mine," I said holding them side by side in front of his face. "Either they are paying her too much, or you are paying me too little," I said.

GGG doubled my salary overnight.

Arlene and I wasted no time starting a family. In the spring of 1957, she got pregnant with our son Jay. She quit her job four months into her pregnancy and stayed home to prepare for the baby. Preparing for a newborn brought back a flood of memories of the siblings and family I had lost. I reflected on how my parents must have felt knowing that their own children might not survive. I didn't know how to handle all the feelings that fatherhood provoked in me. I seldom talked to Arlene—or anyone else for that matter—about what happened to me in Auschwitz and Buchenwald. A part of me died in those camps. I wanted to keep the demons buried. Still, waves of emotion kept crashing over me.

That year during the High Holy Days, I sat Arlene down. "It's important to me that you know how happy you've made me," I told her, putting my hand on her pregnant stomach. "It's the first time in all the years since I was separated from my parents and siblings that I'm with my own family on the holidays. I cannot express how happy that makes me and how much I love you." We held each other and cried.

Even in the midst of my newfound happiness, however, I hadn't completely escaped the Holocaust. "Honey, I need to ask you something," Arlene said before the baby arrived. "It's about your sleep."

"What is it?" I asked.

"Are you having nightmares?"

"I'm fine."

"Honey, you're not fine. Sometimes you wake me up speaking Hungarian or Yiddish. I don't know what you're saying. Your face contorts, your fists clench."

"It's nothing. I'm fine."

"I asked the doctor about it."

"You did what? Why would you do something like that?"

"I'm worried. He said to leave you alone and not to wake you, because then you'd just resume whatever nightmare you were having."

"See. I told you. I'm fine."

"Talk to me, please. I love you. I'm your wife. I want to help you."

I sat in silence and tried to muster the courage to purge the truth. "I love you," I said. "That's why I don't tell you about my dreams. It's too dark, too ugly."

"But I want to know. Please. Tell me so I can understand."

"You can't understand. No one who wasn't there can understand. I hope no one ever has to understand."

"But I see and hear you struggling at night. It's awful. I want to reach inside your dreams and make it stop, but I don't know how. What do you see at night?"

It was time she knew. I took a deep breath. "I'm in the woods. Running through the woods. You and the baby are with me. The Nazis are hunting us. They've got their guns and they're running through the trees, over the rocks, everything. You and the baby are crying. I'm trying to keep you both quiet so they don't kill us. I then do what my father did to me: I split us up. That way the Nazis will chase and kill me but not you and the baby."

I looked up at Arlene. Her face was soaked in tears. She stroked my hair gently with her hand. "Darling, I love you more than you will ever know. I'm so sorry. So sorry. You make me so proud. You are the most wonderful man and husband. You're going to be an incredible father."

"I will always protect you and our family. Always," I said, crying into her chest.

"I know you will, honey. I know."

Jay arrived February 5, 1958. Our second son, Tod, was born on April 23, 1960. I cried the first time I held each of them in my arms. To have my very own sons, to hold them close against my heart, to watch them sleep—it was the fulfillment of my greatest dream for a family all my own, one to cherish and protect.

Building a family was one thing, building a career in men's fashion another. The longer I worked at GGG, the more I realized the importance of cultivating a celebrity clientele. In those days, the entertainment industry's biggest stars wore GGG. Agents and industry executives typically sent celebrities to the main GGG office, not the factory, to be measured, so I had little interaction with them. I wasn't a front man or star salesman like Morris. My hidden role as a tailor afforded me few if any opportunities to build relationships with our A-list clients. One star, however, came directly to the factory for fittings, and it was he who opened the door for me to the Hollywood elite.

Edward Israel Iskowitz, better known by his stage name, Eddie Cantor, was one of America's most beloved entertainers. After scoring early success in Vaudeville, Eddie parlayed his singing and comedic talents into a major career in radio, television, and movies. Eddie knew everyone. He had appeared on Broadway in the fabled *Ziegfeld Follies*, performed with the legends Will Rogers, Jimmy Durante, and W. C. Fields, coined the name for "The March of Dimes," and served as the second president of the Screen Actors Guild. By his mid-thirties, Eddie Cantor was already a millionaire.

Despite his meteoric rise to stardom, Eddie's childhood was tragic. His parents were Russian Jewish immigrants. Eddie's mother died during childbirth when he was one year old. The very next year, his father died of pneumonia. As he put it in one of his bestselling books, *My Life Is in Your Hands*, "I have always felt like a part of other people and that other people were a part of me. The dim, brief images of my father and mother have formed an unforgettable picture in my mind, although I never really had the opportunity to know them or even to speak to them, for as my lips were forming into words they were gone."

Eddie's grandmother Esther Kantrowitz raised him in New York City. A school form accidently listed Eddie's last name as his grandmother's, which an administrator altered to Kanter. Hence, the Hollywood creation of Eddie Cantor.

In their youth, Eddie and Mannie Goldman were among the first to attend Surprise Lake Camp, a nonprofit camp for Jewish boys. Poor boys like Eddie were admitted for free. Rich boys like

Mannie paid full freight. Both men said the camp made a tremendous influence on their lives and taught them enduring life lessons. In the 1920s, Eddie asked Mannie to serve as treasurer of the Eddie Cantor Camp Committee to help support Surprise Lake Camp and other youth programs. As Eddie explained in his book, "Mannie, who, with his brothers, runs the GGG Clothing Company, is the best possible choice for treasurer because any time we're stuck for funds he digs into his own pocket to refill the treasury." He added, "He's been so busy doing, he's never gotten around to marrying and having a family of his own. He's part of my family."

Eddie wasn't joking. In 1938, Mannie and Eddie traveled together to Europe on a fund-raising trip to raise money to help extract refugee children out of Germany. Mannie called in a few fashion-industry chits and set up a meeting between Eddie and Sir Montague Burton, who ran the largest clothing manufacturing business in the world. The connection proved lucrative and made the charity a mint in donations.

On another occasion, Eddie and Mannie met a seventeen-year-old pianist named Hilda Somers, whose fingertips had been severely scorched when the Nazis marched into Austria and forced her to wash the streets with lye. Hilda was brought to live with family in the Bronx. Mannie and Eddie devised a way to get the girl a Steinway piano and a world-class teacher. After one week of lessons, the teacher called Eddie and said she was good enough to play Carnegie Hall with the New York Philharmonic. "I called Mannie and I told him what Carnegie Hall would cost," wrote Cantor. "'So what?' he said. So eventually we presented Hilda at Carnegie Hall with the New York Philharmonic and from there she went on to a series of concerts across the country, ending in a blaze of glory at the Hollywood Bowl. And she's still playing and she's happily married. A cheerful ending to the story that started so sadly in Austria. This is the sort of thing you do when you're palling around with Mannie Goldman."

The parallels between Eddie's and my orphaned childhoods were unmistakable. He had a huge heart and genuinely loved to help people and brighten lives. At the GGG factory, an Eddie Cantor visit was an event. The Goldman brothers would let all 565 employees take a break from work and gather around the big cutting table. Eddie would then hop up on top of the table and do a few minutes of his song and dance routine, which never failed to receive a rousing response.

Despite his fame and fortune, Eddie lacked pretense. He was comfortable in his skin. When his bug eyes earned him the nickname "Banjo Eyes," Eddie owned it and made it one of his comedic trademarks.

I felt a deep and instant connection the first time Mr. Goldman and Mr. Rosenberg introduced me to Eddie. He was firmly committed to the cause of Israel—it was literally his middle name. He took a special interest in survivors, asking questions and listening with a sympathetic and focused ear.

Eddie also loved to test limits. Songs like "Makin' Whoopee" and "The Dumber They Come, the Better I Like 'Em," caused a stir. So, too, did Eddie's embrace of black entertainers of the era. While hosting *The Colgate Comedy Hour* on television in the 1950s, Eddie hugged a young Sammy Davis Jr. and wiped the singer's sweaty brow with his pocket square. The friendly gestures sparked talk of NBC's canceling the show. Cantor didn't care. In fact, he booked Sammy for two more weeks after the incident.

Years later, I measured and dressed Sammy myself when GGG handled the private label for Cy Martin's, a high-end New York haberdashery on Broadway between Fifty-First and Fifty-Second Streets. Perpetually in motion, Sammy filled the room with his charisma. The only problem was that the man wouldn't stand still long enough for me to run a measuring tape around his slender frame. "If you don't stop dancing around, I'm going to have to hold you down to measure you," I warned him.

Sammy said he and I shared the same faith. He explained that our mutual friend, Eddie Cantor, had introduced him to Judaism and had given him a mezuzah, a small scroll bearing a Hebrew verse in a case that is ordinarily attached to a doorpost. Sammy, however, wore his mezuzah on a necklace as a good-luck charm. The one time he failed to wear it, he was in a serious car crash that cracked his cranium and destroyed his left eye. He quickly converted to Judaism. Sammy liked to joke that he was the world's first "black, Puerto Rican, one-eyed Jewish entertainer."

Eddie helped Sammy find God, and he helped Hollywood find me. In early 1960, Sam Rosenberg informed me that he and I would be flying to Los Angeles for a week to attend a men's fashion industry convention. I was honored to be tapped to go on the trip and excited to see a city I had heard so much about.

Several weeks before my West Coast trip, Eddie Cantor dropped by the GGG factory for a fitting and to visit with Mannie Goldman. Eddie and the Goldmans made a quick walk around the factory. "Eddie, I believe you've met Martin Greenfield, GGG's head quality man," said Mannie.

"Great to see you, Martin," said Eddie, shaking my hand.

"Next month Martin here is going to Hollywood to visit all your star pals!" Mannie teased.

"Is that right?" said Eddie. "Who are you meeting?"

"Oh, he's teasing, sir. A few of us are just going to an industry conference in Los Angeles," I explained.

"I see. Well, you know, I'd be happy to set up some dinner meetings for you with Hollywood industry folks if you like," said Eddie. I looked at a grinning Mannie. He always loved to see underdogs get a bigger slice of the pie than they deserved.

"Really? Wow, that would be wonderful," I said.

"Tell you what, I'll have my manager set the whole thing up," said Eddie. "You just tell him the dozen or so actors or entertainers you want to meet and the times you're not tied up with your conference and we'll handle the rest. I'm a member at the Hillcrest Country Club. You can meet them there. We'll take care of it. Okay?"

"Uh…okay," I muttered in dazed disbelief. Eddie flashed his famous smile. "Mr. Cantor, I can't thank you enough, sir. I really appreciate you offering…."

"Don't mention it. My pleasure. Any friend of the Goldmans is a friend of mine," said Eddie.

That night I went home and told Arlene what happened. She couldn't believe it. "Eddie Cantor?" she asked.

"Yes! Eddie Cantor!" I said.

"The same Eddie Cantor that's on the television Eddie Cantor?"

"Yes, that one! The famous Eddie Cantor! He said I could invite whoever I wanted and his manager will arrange the whole thing in Hollywood." We sat in stunned silence in our tiny little Brooklyn apartment.

Eddie's manager called and immediately went to work building a detailed itinerary. "Eddie has several other meetings he would like to set up for you as well, so I'm handling those," said the manager. "You and I will speak every morning to go over the daily schedule. Eddie would also like to speak to you briefly each day to make sure everything is handled to your liking," the manager said. Eddie Cantor knew how to make a nobody feel like a somebody.

"Twelve of the thirteen stars you said you would like to meet with have confirmed they will be joining you at the Hillcrest Country Club for brunch," he said. "The only one who said he can't make it is Eddie Fisher." I didn't like Eddie Fisher anyhow, not after he ditched Debbie Reynolds the previous year for Elizabeth Taylor.

Sam and I put on our sharpest GGG suits. Eddie's manager sent a limousine to take us to our star-studded brunch at the legendary Hillcrest Country Club, Los Angeles's premier Jewish country club and a popular hangout for Jewish celebrities. The limo pulled up to the club and let us out. My palms were slick with sweat. Feeling out of my depth, I dashed into the Hillcrest men's room and stared at myself in the mirror. I didn't belong and I knew it. I was a Holocaust survivor, not a Hollywood star. Nevertheless, I looked the part. My GGG suit matched or outgunned any the stars would wear that day. My attire would have to make up for what I lacked.

I pushed open the men's room door, strode straight into the star-packed dining room, and enjoyed one of the most memorable days of my life. Actors I had seen on the silver screen were now shaking my hand and engaging me in friendly conversation.

Edward G. Robinson, who rose to stardom with his classic gangster roles in *Little Caesar* and *Key Largo*, was there. In more than a hundred films over a fifty-year career, Robinson, a Jew, shared the screen with legends of Hollywood's Golden Age, including Bette Davis, Humphrey Bogart, and James Cagney. The American Film Institute included him in its list of American cinema's twenty-five greatest male actors.

Glenn Ford showed up as well. I had tremendous respect for Ford, who disrupted his acting career to volunteer for the U.S. Marine Corps during World War II. He remained in the Naval Reserve until the 1970s. He played opposite Rita Hayworth in his breakout role in *Gilda* and costarred with Bette Davis in *A Stolen Life*. Ford won a Golden Globe for Best Actor in Frank Capra's *Pocketful of Miracles*. Later, Ford made waves when he campaigned for Ronald Reagan in 1980 and 1984.

I looked around the room and listened to the Hollywood stars holding conversations with one another, punctuated only by the clatter and clink of fine china and silverware. How America had made it possible for me to be in that room, I could not understand. I did my best to pretend I'd been in this situation before.

"Who's up for golf?" one of the stars shouted. "Let's get a group together. How many do we have?"

Robinson nudged me. "You play?" he asked.

"Me? Oh, no. Not golf," I said bashfully.

"That's okay," he said. "You can ride in the golf cart and watch if you like." The rest of the day, I rode around in a Hillcrest Country Club golf cart while our group of Hollywood actors hit the links.

The next morning, right on time, Eddie Cantor's manager called with the daily itinerary, followed by a personal call from

Eddie himself. "How was brunch yesterday at the club?" Eddie asked.

"It was the day of a lifetime," I said. "Thank you so much for making this happen."

"Good. Glad to hear it. Listen, you let me know if you need or want anything else, okay?"

"Yes, sir. I will. Thank you again."

"Have fun out there! I think you're going to like what we have planned for you today."

Eddie's hospitality and generosity were all the more amazing because he had lost one of his five daughters, Marjorie, to cancer the year before. Eddie himself had struggled for years with heart problems. In fact, Eddie called me that day from the hospital.

The driver took Sam and me to the movie set of Bob Hope and Lana Turner's film, *Bachelor in Paradise*. Eddie's manager told us he would escort us to the studio to watch the production. What he did not tell us was that Bob Hope would stop the entire film production and invite us to walk on set and be introduced to the cast and crew. Eddie had spoken directly to Hope and asked him to give us the extra touch. Hope was the consummate gentleman. He didn't appear annoyed or burdened by Eddie's personal request. Instead, he seemed to get a kick out of making us feel important and special.

When he introduced us to the stunning and gracious Lana Turner, I was starstruck. But it was more than that. I was deeply moved by the way accomplished and successful people took time to help someone who could not help them. This uniquely American sensibility of selflessness endeared my adopted homeland to me. I had traveled all over Europe. I'd seen and met all kinds of people.

Americans were different. I had never encountered a people so intent on lifting up individuals. They cared. Best of all, they didn't think it was such a big deal. As Mr. Goldman once told me, "Giving back is fun. The feeling I get back is bigger than the thing I gave."

After almost sixty-five years in the hand-tailored menswear business, I've dressed hundreds of Hollywood actors, scores of celebrities, pro athletes, and business titans, as well as four U.S. presidents and countless politicians—an incredible journey that began with the Hollywood brunch that Eddie Cantor set up at the Hillcrest Country Club.

Irony of ironies, since 2010, Martin Greenfield Clothiers has dressed the Eddie Cantor character played by Stephen DeRosa on HBO's award-winning *Boardwalk Empire*. Martin Scorsese, the series' executive producer, sent his people to my factory to interview me about what it was like to make suits for the real Eddie Cantor. Tod, Jay, and I gave Scorsese's crew a tour and showed them the area where Eddie used to hop up on the cutting-room table and dance and sing for us. I then showed them the kinds of cloth, cuts, and designs we used for Eddie.

Scorsese's people explained that the show was going to be a period crime drama set in the Prohibition era and would include mobsters. "Do you recall ever making any suits for wise guys or mobsters while you were at GGG?" a crew member asked.

"Are you kidding? Of course. Mob guys always made the best customers—they paid in cash," I said.

"Any particular individuals come to mind?" he asked.

"Meyer Lansky," I said.

"The *real* Meyer Lansky? As in, the mobster after whom the 'Hyman Roth' character in *The Godfather II* was patterned?"

"Yes. He wore a 40 short. He was so cautious about security that I never met him face to face. I just made up the suits the way he liked them, and we shipped them to the Fontainebleau Hotel in Miami Beach, Florida."

Scorsese's team liked what they saw and heard so much that we have dressed the *Boardwalk Empire* cast for all five seasons—over six hundred made-to-measure custom jobs, crafted by hand just the way I used to make them for the real Eddie Cantor.

In 2014, I paid a visit to the *Boardwalk Empire* set. They were shooting an episode from the show's final season at the historic Players Club building here in New York. My dear friend Steve Buscemi, who plays the lead character Enoch "Nucky" Thompson on the show, was in the middle of shooting a scene. Watching all the characters shuffle around the period set in our suits thrust me back in time. No matter how many television or movie wardrobes we do, I never tire of seeing my custom creations come to life and dance across the screen. The set and clothes were period perfect.

Ever since Steve appeared in his breakout role in Quentin Tarantino's cult classic *Reservoir Dogs* as the character Mr. Pink, I'd enjoyed watching his career blossom. We always shared a special bond. He's a Brooklyn boy, too. Steve's wife, Jo, often brings their son to the factory, and we have a big time. A man who understands the sacredness of family is one I respect.

Steve's also got a beautiful heart. Before his acting career, he served as a New York firefighter with FDNY Engine 55. When the terrorists attacked America on September 11, 2001, Steve quietly put his acting gigs on hold and drove down to his old fire station to help his brother firefighters pull bodies out of the rubble. When reporters called to ask if the rumors were true, he declined to comment. That's the kind of guy Steve is.

On set, Steve finished his scene and pulled me aside. Unlike some method actors who remain in character in and out of scenes, when Steve's done, he's done; I was talking to Steve, not Nucky.

"How do I look, Martin?" he asked.

I smoothed his lapels and gave him the once-over.

"Beautiful," I said. "Couldn't fit or look better."

"You know the only time I ever heard anyone call me 'handsome' was when I wore your suits," he joked, referencing his trademark quirky look. "Seriously, 90 percent of this role is the clothes. Any time I'm practicing and feeling unsure about a line or scene, I look in the mirror and realize you've already made Nucky. I just have to mouth the words. The suits do the rest."

CHAPTER NINE

THE TAILORS' TAILOR

Hollywood forced me to think and dream bigger.

Hanging out with celebrities boosted my confidence. Stars were just people—nice people, even. Moreover, the menswear conference confirmed that I was on my way to being a master tailor. The industry professionals I met were competent but not superior. My competitive nature let me know I could play with the best—and even beat them. My ego-boosting trip proved timely. As it turned out, Mr. Goldman had bigger plans for my future than I could have ever dreamed.

"We're headed to London, Martino," he said. "Pack your suitcase and bring Arlene."

Mr. Goldman traveled in style and comfort. He never carried money on him save for a single silver dollar. Standing in the hotel lobby, I asked him why he didn't carry cash.

"I don't need to. You don't either," he said. "I just sign for it. If you have any expenses, don't pay for anything. Just tell them you're with Mr. Goldman."

"I don't have to pay them?"

"No. You're with me. That's all you need." Mr. Goldman noticed my confusion. "Let me show you," he said. "Go to that desk clerk and tell him to give you one thousand pounds."

"What? I'm not telling him that. You tell him."

"No, I want you to. Just say Mr. Goldman is your boss."

The experiment made me feel like a stickup artist. When I asked the clerk for the money, not surprisingly, he refused. I then did as Mr. Goldman instructed and told them he was my boss.

"Do you have a check or something?" the clerk asked.

"No, my boss is Mr. Goldman."

"I'm sorry. We don't do business like this in England," he said in an annoyed tone.

Mr. Goldman stepped in. "I'm Mr. Goldman. What's the problem?"

"Sir, I cannot just advance your colleague here *one thousand pounds*."

"Why not? You know Mr. Collette, the famous businessman, don't you?"

"Of course, sir."

"He's my cousin. Call him."

The clerk shot us a skeptical but slightly worried look. While speaking to Mr. Collette on the phone, his expression changed to extreme embarrassment and mortified regret.

"Mr. Goldman, sir, I am so terribly sorry for my mistake.... I...I...I apologize for the misunderstanding, sir."

"Give Martino here the money he requested," said Mr. Goldman.

"Yes, sir. Absolutely, sir. Right away."

Mr. Collette gave us his Rolls-Royce and a driver for the entire week.

Mr. Goldman understood the importance of appearances. He was a master at projecting power and panache. We were suit men. Our business was all about flair and perceived authority. Dress important and you become important. A man who signed for things made an unspoken statement of credit and wealth. Showing up in a Rolls-Royce signaled to prospects they, too, could join the ranks of the elite—or at least look the part—by wearing Mr. Goldman's clothes. Our Rolls took us from haberdashery to haberdashery. Mr. Goldman pitched. I measured. He closed. I learned.

No lesson was too small for Mr. Goldman to impart. When he found out I didn't drink alcohol, Mr. Goldman took it upon himself to set me straight. "If you're going to be in this business, Martino, you have to learn to drink Scotch," he said. He took me to a bar and taught me how to knock back and hold my liquor. I hated the stuff but loved that he took the time to teach me.

Still, even with all Mr. Goldman's one-on-one mentoring, I doubted whether I had it in me to ever become a "front man" in our trade. Mr. Goldman made it look effortless. But he didn't have a foreign accent. Moreover, he had a fancy education and formal sales and rhetorical training. I didn't. I decided it was best to run my measuring tape, not my mouth.

Despite my insecurity about my language and education, though, I knew my value as GGG's virtuoso tailor. By the late 1960s, I had grown frustrated and felt underappreciated. While the company's wealth rose, mine remained flat. Mr. Goldman had told me that if we grew GGG's sales to a hundred thousand units annually, my pockets would be full of cash. After traveling with him to Boston to see Malcolm Kenneth, an outerwear manufacturer, we inked a deal to make their lightweight gabardine coats that pushed us to 110,000 units. I waited two weeks. Nothing. My paycheck stayed the same.

I confronted him. "We are at 110,000 units now. My pockets are empty," I said in a frustrated tone. "I thought you said my pockets would be fat with money if we hit a hundred thousand units. Did you forget that?" The pained look in his eyes let me know my words worried and embarrassed him. The next Monday, he pulled me into his office.

"Martino, you were right," he said. "You're the closest thing I have to a son. I need you to know that. You are vital to GGG's success. From now on, every year, you will receive a substantial annual bonus. There's something else. You're an executive now. That means you represent GGG. So, I'm buying you a new Cadillac with GGG plates. Every three years we'll trade it in and get you a new one in whatever color you want. End of story."

In 1972 Mr. Goldman had a heart attack. I raced to the hospital in a panic. I couldn't lose him.

The nurses made me sit in the waiting room. A few seats over sat a man with a face strikingly similar to Mr. Goldman's, three fat cigars sticking out of his shirt pocket. "Excuse me," I said. "Are you here with the Goldman family?"

"Yes, but my father won't see me," he said. I tried not to let on that I never knew Mr. Goldman had a son. "He disowned me," the man said, tearing up. "But I would like to see him. I really would. But he won't see me." Although I didn't know the story or what had happened between them, my heart hurt for this man I had just met.

I waited until he left before asking the nurse if I could go back and see Mr. Goldman. She escorted me into his room. He was lucid and looked good for having just suffered a heart attack. After a few minutes of small talk, I broached the subject. "Mr. Goldman, you lied to me. You said I was the closest thing you had to a son. But in the waiting room I just met a man who said he is your son. Why did you lie?"

"I didn't lie. He's dead to me."

I later learned the estrangement had been caused by a fight involving stocks and money. I didn't know the details. I didn't need to. The whole thing tore at my heart. The ease with which American families discarded relationships appalled me. It was one of the few facets of American life that disappointed me. People here had no damn clue how blessed they were to live in freedom with their families. That any family could *willfully* and *casually* sever bonds between parent and child sickened me. It was an arrogant, ungrateful affront to God and orphans.

Sadly, over the next few years, the Goldman family's internal tensions intensified. I sensed that serious trouble lay ahead. A high-powered clothing man who had signed deals with Pierre Cardin and Yves Saint Laurent to produce their labels approached me with an offer to join him in a new company. He offered me a one-third stake in the company if I would set up and run a new factory he would build to my specification. The opportunity excited me, but the thought of abandoning Mr. Goldman left me feeling queasy and disloyal. I dreaded telling him.

"Mr. Goldman, I lost my father when I was a boy in the camps. You are like my father. It's hard for me to tell you the story, but now is my opportunity to go into business. To go out on my own. I need your advice. If you were my age and in my place, what would you do? You've never steered me wrong. I trust you completely."

"I am not the best man to ask. I'm an old man—and you're my business! If you don't want to be here, I want to close up the factory. There's no use keeping GGG open if you go." His words stabbed me like a dagger. "Martino, listen to me. If I give you 5 percent of my corporation, you will own it all one day."

"Sir, that's very gracious of you, but I couldn't accept something like that. Besides, your brothers are younger. I'm close to you, not them."

"Fine. Then let me invest in you. How much do you need in order to stay?"

"I don't know...maybe twenty-five thousand dollars?"

"We'll write it up and get it signed immediately."

Several months later, Mr. Goldman told me he needed to speak with me privately. He said to meet him at a nearby park. When I arrived, he had already arrived and was sitting on a bench. "I want this to remain between us," said Mr. Goldman. "I want you to take over the whole business and run GGG."

"What about Sam?"

"You're my guy. You will do a much better job than Sam. You get along with the workers better. You know my business better than anyone." The idea excited me. He was right. I could do a better job. I wanted to innovate and make changes. "You will earn sixty thousand dollars a year, plus your car and all the rest."

"Who would tell Sam I'm the new boss?"

"You would."

"I cannot do that, Mr. Goldman. You hired him. He's my boss. I can't do that."

"Well, if you can't do that then I can't pay you that kind of a salary."

"What if you let Sam go and I take less money."

"That doesn't work, Martino. I will keep him on but start shifting things to you."

In 1977, exactly thirty years after I arrived in America and found work as a floor boy, I bought the GGG factory at 239 Varet Street in Brooklyn for $100,000. The facility and equipment were mine; the GGG brand was not. I would build a new brand from scratch, step by step, picking the people and systems I wanted. I called it Martin Greenfield Clothiers.

We started with six people. I wanted a business where I touched every suit and served as an architect of the human form. Originally, I envisioned a smaller operation that would turn out a hundred suits a week. My boutique-scale vision died hard and fast. The phone started ringing off the hook. A men's store in Philadelphia named Diamonds wanted us to hand tailor their suits. Then Neiman Marcus called. They wanted me to do trunk shows and handle their made-to-measure clients. The suits would have Neiman Marcus on the joker tag but would be hand tailored by us.

My newfound creativity and managerial freedom allowed me to set up smarter systems and do things right. I refused to compromise. We would use only the highest-quality materials and methods. My suits would feature my hand-shaped full-canvas fronts, Italian and English woolens and cashmeres, handmade horn buttons affixed with a smart button stance, endless hand pressing to mold the jacket's form, hand-stitched and functional buttonholes, and collars with a gorge done right to ensure a snug fit around the shirt collar. And above all, only over my dead body would any suit made by Martin Greenfield *ever* feature fused or glued interlining.

A suit jacket has three layers of fabric: inside, outside, and an interior canvas layer. In a handmade suit, the interior layer floats freely between the inside and the outside. That's what gives a jacket verve. Cheap suits fuse or—heaven forbid—glue the middle layer to the front layer. The result is a disgusting mess of a suit. When I'm walking down the sidewalk and see a fused or glued jacket, I cross the street so I don't have to look at it. It's a rumpled, misshapen sartorial atrocity. That doesn't happen with properly constructed free-floating canvas. Not the way I do them. My suits *drape* the body.

In addition to setting soaring manufacturing standards, I also insisted that Martin Greenfield Clothiers' private clients receive a personalized customer experience. It made good business sense, but it made even better tailoring sense. One of the many advantages of a custom suit over a ready-made suit is that I am able to correct for a customer's physical imperfections or irregularities. Uneven arms? I correct for them by modifying the sleeves. Longer-than-normal torso? I change the drop and button stance. Drooping shoulder? I reconstruct the shoulders and make them symmetrical.

I also insisted that we understand each customer's way of life and professional work. For example, when we dressed a Walter Cronkite, Conan O'Brien, or Stone Phillips, we wouldn't use the same fabrics that we'd use for a professional athlete like LeBron James, Patrick Ewing, or Shaquille O'Neal. Television cameras hate certain patterns and sheens, whereas athletic, muscular bodies hate tight seams. I was determined to make sure that the corporate culture of Martin Greenfield Clothiers put a premium on personalized customer communication.

Despite my confidence in my tailoring and systems, I was still insecure about my ability to sell directly to customers. It was a skill I had never had to learn—and wasn't sure I could. Then, in 1978, I got a call from the legendary Stanley Marcus, owner of Neiman Marcus. He wanted me to meet him at his Dallas store for a tuxedo trunk show. "Do up a dozen tuxedos. Give me your very best cuts and looks. I'm flying you down here for a VIP trunk show," he said.

I hadn't liked Mr. Marcus the first time I met him. Worse, I thought he was a Communist. That first encounter was at a men's fashion convention in Manhattan during my GGG days. "Take every penny out of the man's pocket when he shops with you," he had told me. The words made me wince. It reminded me of something the Russian Communists I fled from might say. But then I listened to the rest of Mr. Marcus's spiel:

> When you dress a man, you have to make sure you dress
> him 100 percent. You have to sell him everything he

needs to dress properly. A scarf, a hat, gloves, pocket square—everything. Why? Because if you forget to sell him a pocket square, he's going to run to another store and buy one. That salesperson is going to say, "Do you have a jacket to put it in?" When the customer says, yes, I bought it from Neiman Marcus, the salesman will say, "I can sell you a suit just as good for less." And then you just lost a customer for life—and all because you failed to sell him a stupid pocket square.

A natural-born seller, Mr. Marcus knew what he was talking about. He hadn't built one of fashion's most successful stores by accident. As he liked to say, "I have the simplest taste; I'm always satisfied with the best."

And now Mr. Marcus was calling me to do a Friday night trunk show for him. I made up my twelve sharpest tuxedos and flew to Dallas. Mr. Marcus arranged for a white stretch limousine to bring me to his downtown store, where I was greeted by a big sign out front—"Welcome, Martin Greenfield!"—and chilled champagne at the door. The event was to be a black-tie affair. After greeting me, Mr. Marcus told me to hurry up and change and then come find him before the show started.

That's when he dropped the bomb on me. "I want to switch it up a little tonight," he said. "I will make a few remarks and introduce you, but I want you to get on the stage and sell them." My stomach churned.

"Mr. Marcus, I don't talk. I'm a tailor. You're the salesman. I just know how to make the clothes, not sell them."

"No, I want you to go up there, take a tux jacket, and walk them through all the craftsmanship and tailoring you put into making a suit jacket."

"Mr. Marcus, sir, I don't want to embarrass you. I don't think this is a good idea. I just...."

"Nonsense. You'll do great. Just talk about the quality and details you pour into everything you make. That's all you have to do. Your work speaks for itself. Just show them what you do."

I was so nervous I thought I was going to vomit on the tuxedos. I got in front of the wealthy crowd and went through each section of the jacket, stitch by stitch. I talked about the lining, the seam work, the fabrics—everything. While I was droning on about the workmanship in each coat, Mr. Marcus stood up and interrupted me mid-sentence. "Hey, Martin, I thought you said you couldn't talk? Now stop talking. You already have three guys sitting next to me who are ready to get measured and buy tuxedos. Hurry it up, will you?"

The crowd burst out laughing. I did too.

The three men who wanted tuxedos turned out to be Mr. Marcus's brother, cousin, and son. They may have genuinely wanted the suits, but Mr. Marcus no doubt encouraged them to take the lead so others would follow.

The next day, Mr. Marcus flew me to his Houston store for one-on-one sessions with a few of his top clients. The first man they brought in had his wife with him. She picked out eight tuxedos. "God created the world in seven days," I said. "What do you need eight tuxedos for? I will make you seven and we will talk about suits."

The Neiman Marcus people weren't very happy with me for that. But I wanted clients to know they could entrust their wardrobe and style to me. Just because someone is rich doesn't mean he's content to pay more or get a bad deal. In my experience it's just the reverse: the richer a man is, the more cautious he is about overpaying or being taken advantage of.

Neiman Marcus rounded out my three-city tour with a stop in Florida. From then on, Mr. Marcus had me on the trunk-show circuit handling Neiman Marcus's private-label handmade suits. The relationship with Neiman's was made all the more special by the friendship I developed with the legendary Derrill "The Doctor" Osborn, Neiman's vice president of men's tailored clothing. Derrill's vivacious personal style and penchant for handcrafted quality made him an industry standout others followed. So, naturally, the suits we made for Neiman's caught the eye of Derrill's former employer, Saks Fifth Avenue, who called us to do their private label. Then Barneys New York called, followed by Brooks Brothers, who wanted us to make its Golden Fleece collection. I didn't mind not having my brand name on the inside of the jacket. My signature was the quality that was hand sewn into the suit itself. That's why all the biggest American suit stores came knocking and still do. They know that in the nearly seventy years I've been in the business, we've never once cut corners on quality. We never will.

Despite our rapid expansion and success, I knew I'd need help I could trust to make sure Martin Greenfield Clothiers grew to scale successfully. So I brought both my sons on board. My eldest son, Jay, played tennis at Tufts and graduated magna cum laude. After entering dental school, he took a leave of absence and never returned to graduate, preferring to join his well-dressed father at the factory in 1981. Jay brought business leadership skills along with a strong will and determination to succeed. He quickly became the most knowledgeable piece goods expert in our industry and was instrumental in implementing computerization of our pattern making and design. His vision has helped guide us through the many changes necessary to succeed in our ever-evolving industry.

My other son, Tod, is a creative genius. It took a few years more, but Jay and I eventually wooed him away from his career as a stagehand to join us in 1985. Blessed with superb analytic powers, Tod unscrambled the art of tailoring and made it the science of tailoring. He is the only person I've encountered who can not only copy the tailoring techniques but understand and explain them.

When other companies closed up during hard economic times, I had two energetic, educated secret weapons no one else had. I'm proud to work as a trio with Jay and Tod to create a label that means success. Bringing my sons into the company was one of the smartest business decisions I've ever made. One of the most meaningful, too.

Sometimes, early in the mornings or just before we turn off the factory lights at day's end, I look across the old creaky wooden factory floors, over all the bolts of fabric, around the spools of thread. I spot my sons without their seeing me. I live for those moments. They remind me of all the glances I cast across the Nazi separating room all those years ago in my futile quest to find my father. To know that my boys will never experience that frantic feeling, to have them always near me, to experience the joy of watching them grow in their roles as fathers, husbands, and businessmen, to savor every day in spite of the busyness of modern life—it's my everything.

～✺

Producing stock for major retailers was one thing. But when top designers started asking me to help bring their sketches to life, I knew we had reached a new level of success.

Designers are dreamers. Tailors are makers. I never wanted to be a designer, only a maker. Design is a skill I deeply respect, but I have always found greater excitement in the challenge of building and constructing the suit, in turning the designer's sketches into reality.

The design possibilities for men's suits are far more limited than in women's *haute couture*. To be sure, men's suit styles evolve, but the changes are not nearly as radical as in womenswear. Even so, a quarter inch can completely alter how a man's suit fits and feels.

Between "leisure suits" and Nehru jackets, working with designers has sometimes been a nightmare. Inelegant designs that defy the laws of physics are a waste of time and fabric. I'm all for innovation and experimentation, but only in ways that enhance, not debase, the wearer's silhouette and style. As the late, great Coco Chanel put it, "Fashion passes, style remains." I stand with style.

Fortunately for me, I've had the privilege of working with some of America's greatest designers. When the chemistry is right between a designer and a suit maker, the results can be pure magic.

That was certainly the case in my decade-long collaboration with the legendary Donna Karan. In the 1980s and '90s, Donna helped shatter the menswear glass ceiling for female designers. She won multiple Coty American Fashion Critics' Awards, as well as numerous Council of Fashion Designers of America (CFDA) prizes in womenswear, including their Lifetime Achievement Award. But it was Donna's 1992 CFDA Menswear Designer of the Year Award and the smashing sales success of her men's Couture line, featuring her signature crepe suits, that made it clear menswear was no longer solely the realm of male designers.

My first encounter with Donna was in 1989. We received a call at the factory telling us to expect a delivery from Donna Karan. A young man walked in carrying an Armani suit. He said Mrs. Karan's husband, Stephan Weiss (now deceased), liked the suit. She wondered if I might make him one like it.

"I am not going to copy an Armani suit for Donna Karan," I told him. "I need to speak with Mrs. Karan. Get her on the phone." Startled, he did as I asked. "Mrs. Karan? Martin Greenfield. How are you?"

"Good. And you?"

"I'm great. Listen, why do you want your husband to have an Armani-style suit? If he likes Armani, let him buy Armani. Why not give him a Donna Karan men's suit with a Donna Karan look? Let's create something different together. It should be your style, your look."

She liked that. I brought my in-house designer to the meeting. "Give me your best model and your best fabrics," I said. Donna has an exacting eye for texture and fabrics. She knows what she likes and what works. I appreciated and respected her tenacity and confidence.

"Martin, I'm really liking wool crepe," Donna said. "Blue or black, but definitely crepe."

"Great, let's go with the crepe."

A lot of drawing, a lot of tweaking, and before you knew it, we had hammered out a design. We made up a design sample and returned to Donna's office to go over it. After a few changes—Donna gives incredible attention to even the smallest detail—we had a strong sample. "I'm telling you, this suit is going to sell," I said.

"Let's hope so," she said with a smile.

Donna gave Freddy Pressman at Barneys New York a first-year exclusive on the Donna Karan Couture men's suits. We couldn't make them fast enough to keep up with demand. For years, we made ten thousand suits a year for Donna's line. We also hit the trunk-show circuit together. She was a powerhouse. I saw her score a million-dollar day in a single trunk show at Bergdorf Goodman.

In 1992, Donna was nominated for CFDA Menswear Designer of the Year, the "Oscars" for designers. Before the awards ceremony, Donna, Giorgio Armani, and I chatted. Giorgio, who prefers to speak in Italian but spoke in English for our benefit, motioned for Donna to lean in to hear what he had to say. "The man next to you makes the best crepe suits in the world," he said, loud enough to make sure I heard him and with his characteristic graciousness. "I wish I could make them the way Martin makes them."

That evening, Giorgio presented the Menswear Designer of the Year Award to Donna. I was so proud of her. Our industry can be brutal, but she never waivered. Hard work and heart seldom lose. When Donna took to the stage to deliver her acceptance speech, her eyes found mine. "My father in heaven sent me Martin Greenfield. Thank you, Martin."

Donna's words touched my heart and soul in a way only a child who has lost a father can appreciate. You see, her father, Gabby Faske—also a New York tailor—died tragically in a car crash when Donna was just three years old. There's an unspoken connection only the fatherless can feel. To hear her recognize that tender tether from the dais that night was a blessing I treasure still.

⁓

Another award-winning American design talent I had the privilege of helping was the youngest-ever inductee into the Fashion Hall of Fame, Alexander Julian.

Alex came to us in the early 1980s wanting to bring his passion for bigger suits, fabric design, and bold colors to life. In 1981, he launched his preppy "Colours by Alexander Julian" line and was the first American designer to design his own cloth. His textile designs, inspired by Monet, are so exquisite you could frame and hang them in a museum. And that's exactly what the Smithsonian National Design Museum did as part of its permanent collection.

In addition to his bold approach to color and textiles, when I think of Alex I think of one word: "shoulders." He helped shift the style of men's suits in the 1980s into exaggerated shoulders. The aggressive move caught me off guard the first time he asked me to do it. "Here's what I want: I need you to put a size 46 shoulder on a size 40 suit," Alex told me.

"Say that again," I said.

"46 shoulder on a 40 jacket." My expression must have conveyed my bewilderment. "I know it's different," he said. "That's why I want to do it."

"I understand. I'll give you exactly what you want."

I delivered the 40 suit with the 46 shoulders as promised. Alex was exaggerating his shoulder widths to make a statement. Once he made his point, he could step back a bit with a more moderate, yet still larger, shoulder design.

"Now that you got what you asked for, how about we do something more commercial?" I said, seeing a future in the trend. And we did. Alex's provocative move paid off. He pushed the needle in the direction of bigger shoulders, an evolution that became one of the decade's design hallmarks.

Alex's sudden rise took many by surprise. Before turning thirty, he won his first Coty Award—then considered one of fashion's most prestigious honors. He went on to win four more. In his 1983 Coty Award acceptance speech, Alex paid homage to our partnership. "I'd like to you to meet my maker," he said. "Martin, please stand."

I was touched that he called me his "maker" instead of his "tailor." That's what I consider myself, someone who makes beauty out of cloth.

Alex took advantage of his momentum to nudge the fashion industry in America's direction, and by the middle of the decade he moved his production from Italy to the United States. He was also the first fashion designer to work on professional athletic uniforms, creating a unique teal and purple argyle pattern for the Charlotte Hornets. Before the team's recent rebranding, Alex's design produced a staggering $200 million in Hornets merchandising. How much of that did Alex get? Zero. A true blue Carolinian, Alex had famously volunteered his services to then-owner George Shinn for free, with one proviso: Shinn had to ship five pounds of

Carolina barbecue—or as Alex calls it, "Carolina caviar"—to his place in Connecticut.

I experienced Alex's generosity several times. When he designed the racing uniforms for the legendary Mario Andretti, Alex invited Tod and me to the Meadowlands as guests of Newman-Hass Racing. We were there to measure Mario for suits before the race. Joining Mario, Tod, and me to watch the race was fellow gearhead and Hollywood icon Paul Newman. A short time later, Paul came to Brooklyn to tour our factory and be measured. Paul was the consummate gentleman. He walked the wooden floors and took time to speak personally to my craftspeople. Through the decades we've had countless stars in the factory, but it always stood out to me when a celebrity took time to speak to a stitcher or take interest in a presser. Dressing powerful people has taught me that the greatest men take interest in the smallest people.

That was Paul. We became very close. When he came to me, he was a casual guy who wore old-fashioned sweat suits. But then I dressed him up and he loved his clothes. Once he called me frustrated about the movie industry. He vented and said he was finished with the film business. "I'm tossing my suits in a bonfire, Martin. I'm done and never looking back," he said.

"You are going to still need those suits, Paul. Trust me. I know you're frustrated right now. But life has a way of changing. You will return to the movies. Wait and see."

Sure enough, even after the smashing success of his charitable Newman's Own food company, Paul continued acting and was nominated for an Academy Award for his 2002 role in *Road to Perdition*. Each time I spoke with him, he thanked me for talking him out of setting his clothes on fire. "That would have been one hell of an expensive bonfire," he quipped.

It's unlikely I would ever have met or dressed Mario or Paul had Alex not made the introductions. Great friendships are like great tailoring: the stronger the stitch, the longer it lasts.

One of the great joys of my career has been helping and mentoring young designers. It's one of my passions. Some people have warned me not to do it for fear that an unscrupulous designer might steal my trade secrets. Life is too short to horde your gifts. Knowledge shared extends and illuminates the arc of design history. So when young upstart designers like Calvin Klein, the late Perry Ellis, and Isaac Mizrahi came on the scene, I lent a supportive hand.

I knew Calvin before he was "Calvin." I always believed he would be great. But Calvin faced that early cash crunch that stymies many a young designer. He cared about technique and tailoring. He'd bring me designs and we'd make him samples. Calvin wouldn't just look at the outside of a sample. He'd ask questions, make me explain why and how a seam or vent had been made. In short, he was curious, creative, and teachable—three of the most important qualities for any aspiring fashion designer.

After Calvin solidified his financing, he called me up and proposed a partnership. It was right around the time I'd begun working with Donna Karan, and I told him I'd already pledged my time to Donna's Couture line and was worried that taking on both her and his lines at the same time might stretch us too thin and threaten the quality of our work. The perfect gentleman, Calvin appreciated my honesty and understood completely. His massive success never surprised me.

One person I wish had lived to see his own success was Perry Ellis. We worked with Perry in 1982 to help him create his Perry Ellis Signature collection. He always listened, never insisted, and was comfortable in his own skin. Perry Ellis Signature did well until the designer's deteriorating health prevented him from participating in its promotion. A kind, intuitive man with a good heart, Perry left us too soon.

Another young designer I had fun helping in the '80s was Isaac Mizrahi, a good Jewish boy from Brooklyn whom I naturally wanted to help. With his energy and zany sense of humor, Isaac was fun to be around. His background was more in womenswear, though, so we worked closely with him on producing his Mizrahi New York men's collection. He's gone on to do commercial deals with large retailers like Target.

The fashion press often asks me whether I'm optimistic about the direction today's top young designers are steering menswear. I answer with a resounding "Yes!" The brightest design lights have begun a fearless march back to quality, sumptuous fabrics, and hand-tailored designs. It's classic scarcity. The less frequently customers experience something superior, the more they crave it. Humans spend more hours hooked to machines each day than they do sleeping. This reality has created a ravenous demand for garments made the way only human hands can. Smart young menswear design houses know this and are blending new-school designs with old-school hand-tailored quality.

Two new brands that have cracked the code on quality are Scott Sternberg's Band of Outsiders and Marcus Wainwright and

David Neville's rag & bone. Scott won the 2009 CFDA Menswear Designer of the Year Award. Marcus and David took the prize in 2010.

Scott launched his Los Angeles–based Band of Outsiders in 2004. The next year he visited me in Brooklyn and met Tod, Jay, and my patternmaker, Mario. Scott understood something many emerging designers miss, the power of timeless American classics. He brought a new-school zest to classics like schoolboy blazers and slim suits with narrow lapels, natural shoulders, high armholes, and handcrafted detailing. His background in photography and cinema trained his eye to appreciate subtle beauty. Smart.

The other thing that struck me about Scott was his humble yet certain sense about where a design should go and what it should achieve. He never apologized for his lack of formal design training. Better still, he never tried to fake it—something I can sniff out as fast you can say gorge, button stance, or besom.

In one of his early emails to Jay, Scott included some basic suit sketches of a smart-looking sample we were working on with him. Here's part of what he had to say:

> i hope this finds you well. it was a pleasure to meet you, your brother, dad, mario, etc. and i'm excited to work together moving forward.... attached are some flat sketches with notes.... after this fitting, i would want the final suit made in the correct fabric (on the way from italy), and two blazers made from the vintage woolens i mentioned.... i'm not a technical designer, so if you see something on the flat [sketches] that seems odd, don't think i'm

trying to convey anything more than a small detail. more about the general idea for now. slim! slim! slim!

No pretense, a sure vision, and a commitment to details that matter and quality that endures. I know designers who couldn't write a missive that clear and confident if they had a lifetime to do it. In my book the kid was a winner. The industry and Band of Outsiders' growing customer base agree.

In a business that demands credit for the most minor of innovations, Scott did the opposite. He insisted we include a hangtag on each suit stating it was hand tailored at the hundred-year-old factory of Martin Greenfield Clothiers—a classy move and stroke of branding genius.

The same can be said for my rag & bone boys, Marcus and David—two brilliant Brits I love working with. They got in touch in late 2006. In September of the next year, they invited us to attend their 2008 spring collection show. The rest is history.

Few things excite me more than young designers who are serious and passionate about craftsmanship. That's Marcus and David. They love what they do, and it shows in the way they do their homework, remain true to their English design impulses, and always mind the details and do the work.

In addition to handling rag & bone's made-to-measure clientele like Jimmy Fallon, the boys have us take care of fitting their own suits. It's the ultimate compliment from designer to tailor. It's also a hell of a lot of fun. A few years back, we were fitting Marcus's and David's tuxedos for the 2009 Costume Institute Gala at the Metropolitan Museum of Art, more commonly known as the Met Ball. They loved their hand-tailored tuxes so much that they asked us to make the actress Lake Bell a matching tux to wear to the event as well.

Marcus and David's commitment to keep jobs and production here in America speaks volumes about the brand they're building and the men they are. Even though they're English, they both married American girls and live here in the States. They strive to look after the home team and take corporate stewardship seriously.

When they took top honors in 2010 for CFDA Menswear Designer of the Year, we couldn't have been happier for them. I expect major continued success from my rag & bone boys.

The tango between designers and makers is an intricate partnership combining whimsy and hard work. Through the decades I've been blessed to dance with many of the best. Together, we choreographed styles and trends that clothed the world's most glamorous and powerful men.

Fashion. It's the dance that never ends.

CHAPTER TEN

DRESSING PRESIDENTS AND POLITICIANS

"**P**olitics is show business for ugly people," or so the old saying goes.

Since my early days at GGG, I've worked hard to make sure America's political power brokers look anything but ugly. That's important. In politics, perceptions become reality. Especially today, when a president's every move reverberates around the globe.

Even in the old days, though, most of the politicians I dressed understood that a leader's appearance represents something much larger than his political views. It symbolizes America herself.

Few of my political clients have understood the power of a fine suit better than those from military backgrounds. I learned about that power myself during my brief service in the Czechoslovakian army. Soldiers wore suits every day, and the importance of maintaining a crisp appearance was pounded into them. They knew an officer's rank and authority by his uniform. Indeed, the relationship between men's fashion and the military is longstanding. Civilian staples like pea coats, khakis, t-shirts—they all started with the military.

One of my first political clients was my liberator and hero, General Dwight D. Eisenhower. After the war, when he needed a civilian wardrobe, he turned to his friends the Goldmans. One day in 1949, Mr. Goldman pulled me aside. "I've got a special assignment for you," he said. "I need you to oversee the production of suits for President Eisenhower."

"Eisenhower?"

"Yes."

"He liberated me! He's not the president, he's a general!"

"No, not the president of the United States. He's now the president of Columbia University. He needs suits. They have to be perfect, and I know you're the man for the job."

"That man saved my life. I will make sure we make him the best suits GGG has ever made!"

I couldn't believe my luck. I'd been given the chance to use my skills in the service of a man who had my complete respect. In my mind, General Eisenhower was a giant. But, according to the measurement card, he was 5 feet, 10 inches and 172 pounds, had a 40-inch chest, wore a size 41 jacket, and had a 36-inch waist. I supervised the making of the suits—watching the buttonhole makers, the pocket makers, the under-collar makers, everyone involved with the process—to ensure that every stitch was flawless. I'd never been so obsessed with a suit order. Nothing could be wrong. Everything, as Mr. Goldman said, must be perfect.

Mannie Goldman, who was close with Eisenhower, would have an idea of what the general thought of the suits. The next time I saw Mannie, I jumped him.

"Well, what did he think?" I asked.

"He loved them. Said they were absolutely perfect."

I'd never been more proud in all my years as a tailor. We dressed Eisenhower throughout his tenure at Columbia University. Any time he needed a GGG suit, pants, vest, anything, the order went straight to me. I followed Eisenhower's political rise closely. His ascension to the White House felt like a personal victory, a confirmation that I was not alone in my admiration of the man whose leadership helped win World War II.

I continued making Eisenhower's suits into his presidency. He was the first president I dressed. But given the Goldmans' personal relationship with him, they got all the face time. If I were going to communicate directly with President Eisenhower, I had to get creative. The Suez Canal Crisis that unfolded in 1956 and 1957 prompted me to do just that.

America's tepid response to Egypt's nationalization of the Suez Canal frustrated me. I didn't like that we were sitting on the sidelines while Britain, Israel, and France were already in the thick of the fight. I believed America needed to send Egypt's president, Gamal Abdel Nasser, a strong response, one that could not be ignored.

Foreign policy expert that I was, I determined that President Eisenhower, the former Allied commander and one of only nine five-star generals in American history, was in dire need of my strategic advice. I wrote him a brief, anonymous note. I knew it would never reach him if I sent it through the mail, so I put it in the outer pocket of a jacket I was making for him (and a duplicate in the inside pocket, in case someone found and discarded the other one). "If you want to end the Suez Crisis, you'll send [Secretary of State] John Dulles on a two-week vacation," I wrote.

A few weeks later, I had another brilliant, penetrating insight into international relations on which the leader of the Free World needed my counsel. So I jotted it down and slipped it into another jacket pocket. This unconventional form of presidential advising continued until the Goldman brothers paid a visit to President Eisenhower at the White House. When they returned, I asked them what he thought of his most recent suit.

"The president loves the suits. But he said someone keeps writing and leaving notes in his jacket pockets. He said there were even letters in the *golf pants* we made him. You wouldn't happen to know anything about that would you, Martino?" said Mr. Goldman with a suspicious glance and a raised eyebrow.

Eisenhower was so amused that he eventually told reporters there was a Brooklyn tailor who kept slipping foreign policy advice into his clothes, and the story became more widely known.

Today, my youthful hubris makes me smile. Looking back, though, my innocent, wide-eyed optimism that an American president would read or care about my opinions was a further reflection of my belief that in America, even the little guy's voice is heard. Ike had dealt with the rookie antics of low-ranking infantrymen all his life. If nothing else, I hope my notes gave him a good chuckle.

∽つ

Military men may know the importance of proper dress, but congressmen seldom do. I once attended a large congressional gathering and didn't see a single member of Congress with a suit that fit properly.

That's why shortly after Gerald Ford became president in 1974, GGG contacted the White House and offered the president a made-to-measure suit. Ford was a star athlete with a great physique and had proudly served in the navy during World War II. His tenure as a congressman, however, had made him a lazy dresser. GGG sent a man to the White House to measure the president, and I started making his suits.

I'd been working late at the factory when two large, serious-looking men in suits rushed up behind me and brusquely escorted me to a vacant storage room. "Excuse me," I said tersely. "Hands off! I was liberated from the Germans! Who are you?" One of the men flashed a badge.

"We're Secret Service, sir."

"But you guys are acting like SS."

"We apologize. We have an important, classified task for the president."

One of the agents pulled out two large rectangular plates made of an unfamiliar material. He rapped the plate with his knuckles. "We can protect the president from the back but not from the front. These are specially designed bulletproof plates. We need you to construct two special vests to fit the president. One of the vests needs to be able to break away quickly and needs pockets to hold and hide these plates. The other needs to be an exact copy that he can change into without anyone knowing the difference."

"What kind of material is this?" I asked.

"We can't say. We also can't leave these with you, so we need you to take all your measurements right now." I measured each plate. They were identical in size and thickness.

"How long do you think it will take to construct the vests?" they asked.

"I don't know…a few days, maybe?"

"That's fine. Thank you for your time," one of the agents said.

I made the bulletproof vest with concealed Velcro straps so President Ford could quickly remove it and slip on the traditional one. I cut two pieces of cardboard the size of the bulletproof plates and slid them into the hidden pockets before sliding the vest onto a sizing mannequin. The vest lay flat against the chest.

President Ford survived two assassination attempts. On September 5, 1975, Lynette "Squeaky" Fromme, a follower of the cult leader Charles Manson, was stopped as she aimed a gun at the president. Seventeen days later, a San Francisco radical named Sara Jane Moore fired a shot at Ford from across the street, missing him by several feet. Had either woman's bullet found its target, the results might well have been fatal. President Ford wasn't wearing the bulletproof vest I designed for him either time.

Donna Karan dressed the first lady when President and Mrs. Clinton entered the White House. Before long, Mrs. Clinton asked Donna for help dressing the president. In particular, the president needed tails for the upcoming Gridiron Club dinner with the elite of the Washington press. Donna contacted Jay, and we went to work.

President Clinton appreciated the roomy comfort and softness of the drape-shaped crepe suits we created. Donna told him that he needed to have me come to the White House to take a thorough measurement so we could begin building him a proper presidential wardrobe. Originally, I was to have a private breakfast with the president and the first lady, but when Mrs. Clinton's father suffered a stroke, she understandably had to cancel the breakfast and left.

We moved straight to the fitting. An aide ushered me up to President and Mrs. Clinton's bedroom. "Wait here. The president should be coming any minute," he said before leaving me behind with the personal valet who was in charge of setting out Mr. Clinton's clothes each day. I looked around the beautifully appointed bedroom and soaked in the moment. I noticed some books on a shelf and walked over to read the titles.

I can't believe this, I thought, running my fingers along the book spines. *You are actually standing in the private bedroom of the president of the United States.*

I'd always heard that the first time you visit the White House, the weight of the history that has been made within those walls impresses itself on you. That was truer for me than most. The decisions made in that White House were the decisions that saved my life.

Still, I had a job to do. If I was to build a wardrobe fit for a president, I needed to know what I was working with. So I did the only thing that seemed logical: I walked to his closet and opened the door. I couldn't believe my eyes. A couple of short leather jackets, more jogging suits than any man needs to own, a ratty old overcoat so ugly I was tempted to throw it away on the spot, and a couple of average, off-the-rack suits. "These are *really* the president's clothes?" I exclaimed incredulously to the dresser.

"Yes, sir," he said.

I knew the Clintons had arrived at the White House with modest means. But this had to be one of the most pathetic presidential wardrobes in American history. I had my work cut out for me. I shut the president's closet and waited for him to arrive. When he entered, I felt flushed and nervous. "Hey there, Martin. Sorry to keep you waiting so long. We were just wrapping up my press conference," said President Clinton in his syrupy Arkansas accent.

"No problem. No problem," I said while shaking his hand.

"You come highly recommended. Donna says you're the best."

I was so nervous and flustered I didn't respond to what he'd just said. "How do you feel being president?" I blurted out. He chuckled. "I'm sorry," I said. "Is that a stupid question? I've made suits for presidents before, but I'm just so excited to meet you." He laughed and smiled some more, and I kept rambling. "I know I will never be a president, because I wasn't born here." I couldn't believe the silliness floating out of my mouth.

The president saved me. "I don't think that's a stupid question. I think it's a great question," he said graciously. "It's a tremendous honor. I'm still getting the hang of it myself."

We made some more small talk and finally turned to fashion. "Let me show you what I'm wearing right now," he said, walking to his closet. I braced myself and tried not to make a face. "What do you think?" he asked. It took everything in me not to burst out laughing. This was, after all, the president of the United States of America.

"Mr. President, what I think is that it's time we give you a presidential wardrobe," I said. "I know you like comfortable clothes. But these things won't do. We have to build a proper and fitting look now that you're the president. Don't you worry. I'm going to fix you up."

"Sounds good."

"I'm going to give you Donna's comfort with a presidential look. Now let's talk about tuxedos. Why don't you like tails?"

"Well, it's not that I don't like them. I've just never worn them—and I'm not sure I really know how."

"So you've never owned a full dress tuxedo in all your life? Not even when you were the governor of Arkansas?"

"No."

"Okay. I will teach you how to wear tails, tie a bow tie—everything."

I spent half an hour measuring all around the president to get the twenty-seven precise measurements I needed to craft a true custom suit. "I didn't realize it took this much measuring to make a suit," he said.

"It doesn't for the kind of suits you've been wearing. But when you put my suits on, you'll see and feel the difference."

"Martin, someone told me you used to make suits for President Eisenhower. Is that right?"

"Yes, sir. He liberated me from Buchenwald. Then I made suits for him."

"Wow, that's great. And what's this about you putting notes in his jacket or something?"

"You see, at that time, I was unhappy about our policy on the Suez Canal Crisis. So I wrote him little notes and stuffed them into his pockets every time I made him a new suit." The president laughed at the recollection. "Mr. President, let me ask you something. Do you watch the talking heads on television?"

"Of course."

"The television shows everything—how the jacket sits, where the collar rests, how everything fits. There isn't a man in my industry who wouldn't give his right arm to be me right now. But if you don't wear these suits right, you're going to ruin my reputation."

"I won't let you down," he said laughing.

"I'm going to show you how to adjust the vest, where the pants should rise, what to do to adjust suspenders to make your pants height appropriate—all of it."

After I finished taking the president's measurements, we spent the rest of the hour going through proper white-tie presentation so he would be ready for the upcoming Gridiron Club gala. As I was gathering my things to go, the president suggested we take a few pictures together. "I can sign the photos and send them to you," he said.

"That sounds great, Mr. President. But my train leaves soon and I want to get back today to start working on your suits."

"It won't take but just a minute," he said, looking around. "Let's see, we don't seem to have a White House photographer around." A kid entered the room.

"I brought a camera, Mr. President," I said, holding it up. "We can have the kid over there take the picture." President Clinton howled with laughter. The boy laughed too. I had no idea what was so funny.

We huddled up and the boy snapped the photo, then handed me the camera.

"Thank you for taking our picture," I said.

"Honored to do it, Mr. Greenfield," the boy said. "Nice to meet you. I'm George. George Stephanopoulos." Several months later I learned this Stephanopoulos fellow was a senior advisor to the president. What did I know? He looked like a little kid. I thought he was a White House page or something.

"Thank you, Mr. President. Thank you for bringing me here," I said with a tear in my eye. We shook hands a final time and I started walking toward Clinton's door.

"Martin...Hey listen, if you ever have something you want to talk to me about, you don't need to stuff notes in my pockets. I'll give you my fax number," he said with a smile. As it turned out, I used that fax number more than once. I sent him instructions on how to tie a bow tie.

As soon as I returned to the factory with the president's measurements, the entire team got to work. The president was a solid 44 long. Within two weeks we had four beautiful Donna Karan ventless jackets with the low-button stance, two pairs of double-pleated pants, and two traditional tuxedos. I also made President Clinton his set of white tie and tails, which he wore to the Gridiron Club dinner. In total, we made over twenty suits for Clinton throughout his presidency. He couldn't believe the results. The suits, which were the first of many he ordered throughout his presidency, fit perfectly but still gave him the stretch and comfort he loved—something only a true hand-tailored suit can achieve.

History interrupted my meeting to fit President George W. Bush.

In 2001, I traveled to Washington, DC, and stayed at the Mayflower in preparation for my trunk show at the downtown Brooks Brothers. I was scheduled to meet President Bush that day for a measuring after he returned from Florida. The date was September 11, 2001.

When news broke of the terrorist attacks on the Pentagon, people flooded the streets and fled the capital. I made contact with Arlene and the boys. Once I knew they were safe and realized that I had no way of leaving Washington that day, I decided to keep the trunk-show date. The next morning I walked to Brooks Brothers. I didn't think any customers would show up, but they did, one right after the other. People deal with fear and grief differently. I suppose it was their way of distracting themselves, of making a small statement that the terrorists would not intimidate them into changing their way of life. Measuring every customer that day, I was never prouder to be an American.

I struggled the rest of the week to find a way home. Eventually, my good friend General Colin Powell stepped in and somehow got me a first-class train ticket to New York. Pulling into Grand Central Station, I felt the sting of tears in my eyes when I saw the gaping hole in the skyline where the Twin Towers had stood majestically just a few days earlier. My heart fluttered the moment I realized that the North Tower of the World Trade Center had been home to the Windows on the World restaurant, many of whose staff I saw regularly and considered friends. I'd experienced loss throughout my life. Like so many other Americans, I never believed evil possessed the ability to turn our buildings into battlefields, civilian airplanes into missiles. I grieved our nation's loss of life and loss of innocence. It was a feeling I knew all too well and had hoped my fellow Americans would never have to experience.

Initially, the Obama White House neither confirmed nor denied that Martin Greenfield Clothiers made President Obama's suits.

It's always been our policy not to comment on whether we dress a celebrity or public figure until he or his representatives mention it publicly. But when former *Washington Post* Style editor Ned Martel wrote a moving profile on me wherein he reported that the White House visitor logs contained Tod's, Jay's, and my names, the connection became public knowledge.

To date, we've made many suits for President Obama. In fact, virtually every suit he's worn since February 2011 has been one of ours. Doing so has been an incredible honor and privilege. The president's aide said he likes the suits so much he doesn't like to travel without them.

It all started in October 2010 with an email Jay received from the legendary Chicago fashion retailer Ikram Goldman, owner of the Ikram boutique. A style advisor to first lady Michelle Obama, Ikram had been asked to recommend an American tailor who could make fine suits for President Obama. She graciously recommended us.

There was one condition, though. The White House said President Obama didn't want to be measured. They would send us one of his suits for us to copy. I told Jay no way. "You write back to the White House aide and say that Martin Greenfield does not copy anybody's suits. Everybody copies Martin Greenfield's suits. You understand?" Ever the diplomat, Jay finessed my message slightly. Still, it worked. We received a note insisting it would be a pleasure to have me come to the White House on November 2, 2010, to measure President Obama for his first Martin Greenfield suit.

No matter how many times I visit the White House, I always feel like a little kid, filled with wonder. Those visits remind me of my first trip to Washington, DC, with Kalvin all those years before. Back then I looked at the White House from the outside. To measure and make suits for the president humbles me.

The first time I met President Obama was in his private office on the third floor of the White House at seven o'clock in the evening. I was struck by his height and smile. He's built like a fitting mannequin, a 40 long with an impressive 33½-inch waist, which makes dressing him extremely enjoyable.

The president showed us a fine Italian-made suit jacket. "Feel this jacket. It's soft and feels really nice. This is the kind of thing I would like you to do for me," he explained.

"Mr. President, this I can do. In fact, it's going to be much, much better than this." He liked that.

He also had some suits from Hart Schaffner Marx, an American company. During the 2012 presidential campaign, the press began comparing the president's suits with Governor Mitt Romney's Hickey Freeman suits and said President Obama's looked better. What they failed to mention was that the suits they were comparing were *our* suits, not Hart Schaffner Marx's.

I wanted to do something special for President Obama's suits. So we developed a special red, white, and blue hand stitching that we use exclusively on the interior linings of his jackets.

Three months after we delivered President Obama's first suits, one of his aides contacted us and said "the boss" loved them so much he wanted us to return to the White House for another order. The president "wears your suits during his special occasions," the aide told us, including a visit to Buckingham Palace.

In March 2012, the White House said the president needed four more suits "right away." President Obama looks great in any color but prefers charcoal gray and navy blue. So we rushed him two of each and shipped them in advance of the White House fitting.

When Jay and our head tailor, Joseph Genuardi, made our company's sixth visit to the Obama White House in February 2014, they encountered a new influence on presidential fashion—the first daughters, Malia and Sasha. "My girls tease me about my suit pants," the president explained. "They say my pleats make me look old and uncool."

"Why don't we make an extra pair of pants in the same fabric for each suit," said Jay. "Only we'll make them flat-front to give them a modern look."

"Let's do that. Then maybe Malia and Sasha will lay off from making fun of me," joked the president.

President Obama said he also needed a sport jacket. "There are several varieties of sport jackets, Mr. President. Do you have a particular preference?" asked Jay.

The president shot us a slightly perplexed look. "I really don't. I'm not sure how to pick the right thing for something like that," he said.

"Any chance the first lady might help you pick one?" Jay asked.

"Well, Michelle never gets involved with my fashion business," he said with a smile.

"Wow, that might be your biggest accomplishment yet. I dress a lot of people and no one accomplishes that!" Jay joked.

In addition to the presidents I've dressed, I've had the privilege of dressing men who might have been president. One such man is my dear friend, former secretary of state Colin Powell. One of his cousins, also a friend of mine, introduced us around the time of the First Gulf War. We first met at a gathering at the Waldorf Astoria when General Powell visited for a parade. "My cousin tells me you're the best tailor in America," said the general. "When I retire, I'll be wearing civilian clothes. I'd be honored if you'd put me in my next uniform."

His first visit to my factory in Brooklyn was deeply emotional. I walked him through all three floors of the building, explaining each station. When we got to the rows of seamstresses doing needlework by hand, General Powell stopped and stared at an older female worker with tears in his eyes. "Martin, I know this work very well," he said. "I grew up in the South Bronx. When my mother came to this country from Jamaica, she worked long, hard days as a seamstress in the garment district."

That moment was the start of a sweet and special relationship that continues to this day. Secretary Powell is much more than a client. I consider him a trusted friend. I've dined at his home. And while I know the White House chefs are some of the best in the world, Secretary Powell's wife, Alma, surely gives them a run for their money.

He's also one of the few Gentiles I know who speaks Yiddish. As a boy, he worked at a toy store owned by a Russian Jewish immigrant. There he picked up several Yiddish sayings, which he loves to use with me. When my name pops up in the press, or on my birthday, a call from Secretary Powell is soon to follow. "Mazel tov!" he'll say, before spending time he doesn't have with me on the phone. He has called me his "mentor." And while I may have taught him a thing or two about the art of dressing, he's taught me volumes about the true meaning of friendship.

He's also been a great referrer of clients. Many of my political clients came to me through my trunk shows at Brooks Brothers in Washington, DC. The events became a magnet for politicos. Every time I came to town, politicians from both parties flocked to the store in a rare display of Beltway bipartisanship. That's what happened with former secretary of defense Donald Rumsfeld—sort of. Secretary Powell told Secretary Rumsfeld he should attend one of my upcoming Brooks Brothers trunk shows and get measured.

"I already wear Brooks Brothers," said Rumsfeld.

"You wear off-the-rack Brooks Brothers. You need to move up to a true custom-made suit by America's greatest tailor," Powell told him.

Rumsfeld called me to set an appointment. "I can't come during the daytime business hours," said Rumsfeld, "because I actually work all day!"

"Ha! I see."

"So you have to either wait for me until evening hours, or we can do it on Saturday when I'm not here working."

Secretary Rumsfeld brought his wife, Joyce, into the shop for his Saturday fitting. "Are you going to make me look like you?" he said, looking at my three-piece suit. "If so, I'm buying." The Rumsfelds were true fiscal conservatives. They refused to ever charge a purchase to a credit card and always paid in cash, which the store appreciated.

Secretary Rumsfeld said he and his wife loved his suit. I knew he was telling the truth, because he came back and purchased more. The secret to selling an important man more suits is to please his wife. Once she sees her husband resplendent in his suit, he's a buyer for life. Or, for the life of the marriage at least. In the Rumsfelds' case, that has worked out. They've been married since 1954.

Another military man with a great marriage who became a client is Senator Bob Dole, whom I first met when he came for a fitting at one of my DC Brooks Brothers trunk shows. The company is an American institution with a great history. If the brand was good enough for the likes of F. Scott Fitzgerald, it's good enough for any American male.

I always enjoyed and respected Senator Dole. As a soldier in World War II, Dole was hit in Italy by Nazi machine gun fire that ripped through his back and right arm. He received two Purple Hearts and a Bronze Star for valor. Despite his miraculous recovery, his right hand was permanently immobilized. Senator Dole reminded me of all those American boys who voyaged across the ocean to fight for the freedom of me and millions more they didn't know. Every time I saw him, I thanked him for his service and told him how grateful I was for his sacrifice. Without men like him, I would have been killed in the camps and never been given the opportunity to live the American dream.

"It was an honor to serve," said Senator Dole humbly. "Privilege of a lifetime." A man like that deserved a great suit. I saw to it that he got one. In addition to precision measurements, I wanted to do something special for Senator Dole's jacket closure to make it easier on him when buttoning his jacket. So I altered his button stance and created a hidden loop that made it easier to fasten his jacket.

Senator Dole's wife, Liddy, who became a U.S. senator in her own right, called me to tell me how much she loved her husband's suit. "Martin, I'd love for you to make Bob another suit," she said.

"It would be my honor."

"I want to give it to him as a gift and make it a surprise," she told me. "Would he need to be measured again?"

"Not at all. I've got his measurements on file. Unless you've fattened him up, we should be good to go."

Later, I saw Senator Dole wearing the suit at an event for the World War II Memorial he did so much to make a reality. I felt proud to see him looking so great while doing so much good.

Convincing political clients to make the leap to made-to-measure elegance was not always so easy, however. Before he became vice president of the United States, then-senator Joe Biden rode the train back and forth from Washington to his home state of Delaware. We bumped into each other frequently and sat together on many a train trip. He's a loud, funny guy. After a few train rides together, I finally got up the nerve to tell Senator Biden the truth. "Senator, I think it's time you let me fix you up with a decent suit."

"What are you trying to say, Martin? What's wrong with the suit I've got on?"

"Well, honestly, it's not that great. Besides, it's time we get you to change from a double-breasted jacket to a single-breasted suit."

"But you don't sell to Democrats! You only dress Republicans!"

"What planet are you living on? I'm an independent suit maker. I dress *many* Democrats."

"Really? I didn't know that."

"I make suits for anyone who has the money to buy them from me."

"Yeah, well, maybe that's why I've never heard of Democrats buying from you. Rich Republicans are the only ones who can afford you."

"I dress Bob Strauss," I said, referring to the former head of the Democrat Party.

"Yeah, well, Bob can afford it."

"I make suits for all the Democrats in Hollywood, too."

"Yeah, well, I don't have that kind of cash."

When Biden became vice president, he called Brooks Brothers and said he needed his suit lapels altered and wanted me to fix him up. "Send it over to me," I told them. "I'll take care of the lapel problem and make sure the whole thing is done right."

To Biden's credit, he finally ordered a Brooks Brothers suit, but it was stock. The vice president had me alter it to make it fit right. It wasn't as good as a genuine made-to-measure, but it was better than off-the-rack.

New York City is famous as the capital of the financial world, but it's also the capital of the fashion world. And few men understood the importance of supporting our industry as well as the former mayor of New York Michael Bloomberg. People always talk about Mayor Bloomberg's wealth and success in business. But to me, the most remarkable thing about him is the way he listens and truly cares. And not in that phony, political way so many politicians do. He really *listens* to what people say.

I saw that side of the mayor during the first of many fittings at my factory in Brooklyn. For nearly an hour, America's eleventh-richest person sat and asked me questions about my time in the concentration camps, listened compassionately as I struggled to speak about losing my family, and even wiped a tear or two from his eyes.

He has my respect.

He also has my suits—lots of them. As the mayor told the *New York Daily News*, he buys all his suits from us. "Every suit," he said. "And they're cheaper than Paul Stewart, where I used to get my clothing." What can I say? The man knows what he's talking about. You don't get to be a billionaire without knowing value when you see it. Just ask another of our billionaire friends, the one and only Donald Trump. Working with Mr. Trump has always been an honor. His larger-than-life style and brilliant business savvy have been a blessing to New York City, creating thousands of jobs. He's a wonderful guy—and a terrific father who understands that life's greatest investment is in one's children.

Everyone knows who Michael Bloomberg and Donald Trump are. But sometimes I've dressed power players without even realizing it. Once, while I was doing a Brooks Brothers trunk show in Washington, DC, a man in a wheelchair rolled in and said he wanted me to make him some suits.

"What do you do for a living?" I asked.

"I'm a lawyer."

"Great. What kind of suits are you looking to buy?"

"Well, I may have some television appearances here in the near future and want to look my best. You come highly recommended, so I was hoping you could fix me up."

"Let me ask you a personal question: Do you always stay in your wheelchair?"

"I'm always in it, unfortunately."

"Not a problem. Not a problem. It's just important for me to know so I can measure and fit you properly."

I made sure to pay careful attention to the drape of his jacket. I wanted to make sure his jacket buttoned flat while sitting to give him a crisp, clean look on camera. "How many suits are we looking to create?" I asked.

"Six."

"Six? Wow, you must really be expecting some serious TV time," I joked, trying to coax him to volunteer more details. He chuckled but said nothing.

Several weeks later, I went home after work and heard a voice I recognized coming from the television in the kitchen, where Arlene was making dinner.

"Arlene," I said, "what are you watching?"

"President Clinton's impeachment trial," she said. I rounded the kitchen corner. There, on the television, was my client sitting in his wheelchair. He was Charles Ruff, President Clinton's chief attorney.

"That my client!" I said.

"Your client is President Clinton's lawyer?" asked Arlene.

"That's the one."

"Well, I must say, he does look sharp in that suit."

Later, I learned that President Clinton had referred Ruff to me. Great salesman, President Clinton.

One of my closest Democratic client friends was the legendary Bob Strauss. The last American ambassador to the USSR and the first to post-Soviet Russia (under the Republican George H. W. Bush), chairman of the Democratic National Committee, Middle East negotiator, cofounder of the powerhouse law firm Akin Gump Strauss Hauer & Feld, recipient of the Presidential Medal of Freedom—Bob did it all.

Strauss was a likeable, straight-talking Jewish Texan whose father had emigrated from Germany and ended up in New York. Bob's mom thought he would become Texas's first Jewish governor. As influential as Bob was, that would probably have been a demotion.

Bob loved fine suits and had more than enough money to afford them. In 1985, he called me a few weeks before President Ronald Reagan's groundbreaking for the U.S. Holocaust Museum. "Get your best suit ready," he said. "I've got you and Arlene front-row seats to the Holocaust Museum groundbreaking ceremony. I've taken care of everything. A limo will pick you two up and take you anywhere you want to go."

"Bob, I don't know how to thank you," I said, my voice cracking.

"Marty, are you kidding? It's my absolute pleasure." He meant it. Bob was the consummate giver. He loved nothing more than to give unexpected and meaningful gifts to his friends. As it turned out, his gift proved far more special than even he intended. During the ceremony, an old rabbi got up to make some remarks. His face looked familiar, but I couldn't place him.

"I know that rabbi from somewhere," I whispered to Arlene. The rabbi continued speaking. He explained that he had witnessed the Nazi atrocities of the Holocaust firsthand as a chaplain in the

U.S. Third Army, which liberated Buchenwald. *No way,* I thought. *It can't be him.* And then, as if God Himself were winking down at me, the rabbi told a story that I knew well. After the liberation, he recounted, a young boy had asked him a question he could not answer: "Where was God?"

"It's him!" I said excitedly to Arlene. After the ceremony, I found the rabbi. "Rabbi Schacter, my name is Martin Greenfield. I was at Buchenwald. I was the little boy who asked you the question."

Rabbi Herschel Schacter told me he lived in the Bronx. We stayed in touch until his death in 2013. Every time we visited, no matter the occasion, we relived the story together. But standing there at the Holocaust Museum dedication, which had turned into a Buchenwald reunion, with tears streaming down our faces, all we could do was hold onto each other. I didn't want to let go of him. He didn't want to let go either. To experience once again that connection, to stand with the man who had held me as a boy when my spirit had been shattered by the Nazis and their lust for death and darkness—I felt as though I'd been kissed by an angel.

CHAPTER ELEVEN

SUIT MAKER TO THE STARS

I n the early years, Kalvin and I were too poor to own a television. The movies, however, we could afford. I learned a lot about America through cinema. Humphrey Bogart, Edward G. Robinson, John Wayne, Gary Cooper, Fred Astaire, Marlon Brando—these actors molded my image of the American male and how he should dress. Even before Eddie Cantor set up my first trip to the West Coast, I'd been captivated by the magic and mystery of Hollywood. That interest only intensified the more I understood the intersection between film and fashion. Celebrities didn't just *want* to look fabulous, it was their *job* to look fabulous—both on camera and off. That made the entertainment industry a promising market for my handmade menswear.

That's even truer now. Today's high-definition movies and televisions put tremendous pressure on directors and costume designers to make sure every stitch is period perfect. Modern audiences are unsparing in detecting and publicizing design flaws.

Period directors and costume designers love our team because we share their passion for accuracy and excruciating attention to detail. We are able to re-create the suit styles of the past because we're among the only companies that practice the handcrafted techniques from a hundred years ago. It's all done right here in Brooklyn.

Mind-boggling amounts of historical and archival research go into world-class costume design. But when it all comes together, the payoff can be exhilarating. That was certainly the case when we worked with the costume designer Catherine Martin, whose husband, Baz Luhrmann, directed the 2013 film *The Great Gatsby*. Catherine got in touch with us in 2011 and asked us to help craft all the suits, vests, sport jackets, formal wear, and slacks for the film's three male leads, Leonardo DiCaprio (Jay Gatsby), Tobey Maguire (Nick Carraway), and Joel Edgerton (Tom Buchanan). Our pattern maker, Billy Hinkle, and my son Jay worked closely with Catherine's team to create dazzling designs true to the period.

Gatsby was shot in Baz and Catherine's home country of Australia, so measuring Leo, Tobey, and Joel took place during a narrow window when all three were in New York for screen testing. I sent Jay to do all the measuring and fitting. While measuring Leo, Jay and Catherine's team got into lengthy discussions about the precise shade for Gatsby's famous pink suit. Catherine also decided that the lining of one of Joel's jackets should feature a Skull and Bones motif as a nod to the character Tom Buchanan's Yale roots.

During a recent fitting in Boston for Joel and Johnny Depp's forth-coming film *Black Mass*, the first thing Joel mentioned was how much he loved his *Gatsby* wardrobe and all the little details. The Skull and Bones lining in Joel's jacket appears in the film only for a blurred second. But the point was that no detail was too small to scrutinize. Catherine and her team were our kind of clothing people.

Originally, we expected that Catherine would want the kind of accurately styled 1920s clothing we had made for projects like *Boardwalk Empire*. But Catherine envisioned more modern suits with 1920s details and styling. I have to admit, I wasn't sure at first that was the way to go. Sticking with the tried-and-true Brooks Brothers designs of the era seemed a safer course. But her instincts proved to be spot-on. When we watched the film and saw Baz's directorial fusion of old-school extravagance and new-school edge, Catherine's vision made perfect sense. The Academy thought so, too. Catherine took home the Oscar for Best Costume Design.

A fun offshoot of our collaboration on *Gatsby* was getting to dress Baz as well. One of the highest compliments a designer or director can pay is to ask you to make clothes for him personally after the designs have been completed for the film. In May 2014, Baz was in town and called to see if we could make tails for him to wear to the 2014 Met Ball. His invitation from famed *Vogue* editor in chief Anna Wintour clearly specified that it was a white-tie affair. Baz needed an incredibly fast two-day turnaround, so we told him to rush over to Brooklyn. It was great visiting with him in the wake of *Gatsby*'s success. Baz was thrilled with the tails we made him and ended up giving Leo a run for his money in the elegance department.

Creating period clothes for films like *The Great Gatsby* is always an exciting challenge. Working with kindred sartorial spirits who share our obsession with hand-tailored perfection makes the process all the more rewarding. One of our longest-running period collaborations has been with HBO's *Boardwalk Empire*, set in Prohibition-era Atlantic City. Terence Winter, the show's creator and one of its executive producers, combines a rare panoramic vision of the project with attention to details. An accomplished screenwriter (twenty-five episodes of *The Sopranos*), he was nominated for an Academy Award for *The Wolf of Wall Street* screenplay. We knew he'd demand the best.

Winter's commitment to precision paid off. *Boardwalk Empire* took home the Golden Globe for Best Television Series Drama. In 2011, Martin Scorsese, one of the show's executive producers and directors, also won an Emmy for Outstanding Directing for a Drama Series. Through *Boardwalk Empire*'s pilot and five seasons, we dressed 173 characters and made over 600 suits. Our work was made much more manageable by the show's talented and hard-working costume designer, John Dunn, who came to us with piles of research—mug shots of gangsters, clothing catalogues from 1917 and 1918 (because people in 1920 would likely have worn clothes from a few years prior), colored drawings and silhouettes from the period (there weren't color photos back then) with the fabric swatches still attached. You name it, John had it.

The jackets of that period, longer and higher waisted, were fitted in the shoulder, as they are today, but featured a natural, rounded shape. Pants were trim in the leg, like today's styles, but had much higher waistlines and button flies. Fabric selection was the hardest part. We searched the world for vintage fabrics, like tweeds and heavy worsted wools, to remain true to the period.

Under John's careful eye, the finished suits impressed even Scorsese. When Jay went to the studio during the filming of the pilot, John approached Jay and said Scorsese wanted to speak with him. "Is everything okay?" asked Jay.

"Oh yes," said John. "He loves everything and wants to tell you so. I'm a little stunned, though, because Scorsese seldom interacts with anyone but his inner crew on set."

Scorsese greeted Jay and complimented him on how beautiful the clothing was. He must have meant it. In 2011, we made suits for another of Scorsese's films, *The Wolf of Wall Street*. When Leo DiCaprio looked in the mirror during a fitting, he said, "My right shoulder looks lower than my left."

"That's because it is," Jay replied matter-of-factly, and kept fitting him.

On other occasions, historical costume design research has hit much closer to home. When we made Denzel Washington's suit for the film *The Great Debaters*, I patterned the styling of Denzel's jacket after the coat I wore in one of a handful of Grünfeld family portraits that survived the Holocaust. It was true to the film's time period, and it worked. Of course, it doesn't hurt that Denzel is a beautiful guy.

Jay, Tod, and our more than a hundred Martin Greenfield Clothiers employees work out of the very same GGG factory I got my start in. I work six days a week. Someone recently asked why I still put in so many hours. "I don't want to miss out on all the fun!" I told him. You see, unlike in the old days, celebrities, directors, costume designers, political leaders, and pro athletes all come directly to the factory for fittings. As one client put it, "I love coming to the factory for my fittings, because I never know whom I'm going to run into."

Rising stars in men's fashion vie for apprenticeships with us. Building a company filled with world-class tailoring talent is one of my greatest accomplishments. It was always my goal to be a faithful steward of the GGG production model that Mr. Goldman imparted to me. That means building young tailors from the ground up and not rushing their training. It takes an extremely dedicated person to make it through the years of hard work we put them through. For that reason, I try to give my talented tailors the chance to interact with celebrities. These opportunities are an important part of their apprenticeship and allow our company to cultivate superior craftsmen from within.

Besides all that, it's also a whole heckuva lot of fun for them. Some of my fondest memories from my early days in the business are of the excitement that came with the chance to meet with stars like the fellows in the Rat Pack. As I mentioned, I met and made GGG tuxedos for Frank Sinatra and Sammy Davis Jr. Well, I say tuxedos—they were technically costume tuxedos. Sinatra and many other entertainers of the era often asked us to make their jackets with no pockets, just dummy flaps. That made their clothes a "costume" and therefore a tax write-off.

Still, in those early days at GGG, access to stars was limited because measuring was done at the business office on Fourteenth Street, not at the factory. On special occasions, however, Mr. Goldman allowed me to offer white-glove service by hand delivering suits to stars. One of those deliveries was to another member of the Rat Pack, Dean Martin, and his costar, Jerry Lewis.

I'd worked for a week making tuxedos for Dean and Jerry Lewis. Like most of the biggest entertainers of the era, they wore GGG. Mr. Goldman informed me that Martin and Lewis would be appearing together at Paul "Skinny" D'Amato's famous 500 Club in Atlantic City, one of the Rat Pack's favorite haunts. Mob guys loved the joint as well.

When I arrived at the 500 Club, I couldn't find Martin or Lewis. I asked a worker to point me to the owner. "Skinny's playing cards in the back," he said. "Go on in." I walked into a small room that looked like a scene out of a movie, with tough men seated around a poker table under a cloud of cigar smoke.

"Can I help you?" said Skinny.

"Yes, sir. I'm here to deliver Mr. Martin's and Mr. Lewis's tuxedos. I'm from GGG."

"Great. Let me see if I can find them," he said getting up from his chair. "Here, kid, take my hand and raise him."

Skinny handed me his cards. In the center of the table sat a big pot of money. I don't recall the exact cards, but Skinny's hand was strong. My competitive spirit kicked in. I figured I could win the pot for Skinny.

I raised.

The other guy raised.

I raised back and held my breath.

My opponent took a long look at his hand—and folded.

"Nice work," one of the men said to me. I raked in the money and started sorting it for Skinny before he walked back in the room.

"You won! Nice going, kid! I couldn't find Dean or Jerry. I'll get them the suits."

"Thank you, sir," I said, disappointed that I wouldn't meet Martin and Lewis after all. "Please tell them if they desire any alterations, Mr. Goldman said we are happy to make them right away."

"Great."

I got up from the poker table and started walking toward the door.

"Hey, where are you going?" Skinny yelled. "You forgot your tip."

I walked back to the poker table.

"That's your money. That's your tip."

He handed me the stack of bills. It was more than I made in a week at the factory.

⁓

Not all our experiences dressing celebrities have had happy endings. The saddest involved a special series of secret costumes we made for the King of Pop, Michael Jackson.

In May 2009, Zaldy Goco, a fashion designer from Chelsea, New York, showed up at the factory. Zaldy was in charge of Michael's costume designs for his This Is It tour. He said he wanted us to create something magical for Michael. And he needed it in a rush. "I need you to make two unique suit costume designs and two backup duplicates," Zaldy explained. "We need them no later than the end of June."

"That's fast, but we can handle it," said Jay. "Get him in here and we'll measure him up."

"That won't work. Michael doesn't do Brooklyn."

"How can we make custom costumes if we can't, well, *measure* him?"

"Simple," said Zaldy. "Michael is my size. You can measure me. If it fits me, it will fit him." Zaldy was rail thin and looked about Michael's height. "Here's what I want to create," he said, laying out sketches.

He needed silk and wool fabrics featuring metallic buttonholes with dangling gold chains. He said the lining should be red and feature pictures of Michael moonwalking. Also, he wanted a blue Italian silk suit with a tapered waist, two inches of shoulder padding, and slanted flap pockets and peak lapels. "Piece of cake!" I joked to Jay.

This was hardly our usual assignment. But then again, Michael Jackson was no ordinary client. The challenge of bringing Zaldy's whimsical design to life excited our team. Zaldy has since gone on to work with Britney Spears, Keith Richards, Mick Jagger, Jennifer Lopez, and many other top musical talents. Judging from the creativity of his designs, it's easy to see why.

We constructed a muslin mock-up. Zaldy flew it to Los Angeles and sent us back faceless pictures of Michael wearing the mock-up. The photos were extremely helpful. They allowed us to modify the design and reconstruct the muslin to better fit his form. Zaldy took the updated muslin back to Los Angeles and flew back with a new set of pictures of Michael wearing the muslin. In early June, Zaldy did yet another cross-country muslin run and returned with yet more faceless photos—eight in all.

In an all-hands-on-deck effort, our team finished two costumes with identical backups and shipped three of them to Zaldy by the middle of June. Michael wore them at a rehearsal two days before he died. The fourth and final suit went out June 26, 2009, just hours after Michael's passing.

We had hoped these would be the first suits we made for Michael. Instead, they were the last.

~⌒⌒

Sometimes films require that we make clothes from less-than-fortunate fashion periods like, say, the 1970s. Take, for example, the 1970s suits we made for Ben Affleck in the Oscar-winning film *Argo*. The film's costume designer, Jacqueline West, wisely didn't allow corny bell bottoms and super-wide lapels to upstage the film's characters. Still, for Affleck's character to look true to the times, we had to create some '70s styles. The suits we made matched the era perfectly but are hardly considered great looking today. Still, I was pleased that Affleck liked the clothes so much he kept them. (Our apologies to Jennifer Garner.)

A similar thing occurred with one of the suits we made Al Pacino for his Oscar-winning role in *Scent of a Woman*. The designer sent cloth for one of Al's plaid suits that was riddled with moth holes. When we pointed the holes out to the designer, she explained that they were intentional. The goal was to make the suit look old and worn. Thankfully, *Scent of a Woman* also featured some gorgeous suits that allowed us to dress Al stylishly. Given the film's famous tango, we took extra care to create a suit that looked spectacular while still allowing Al to move freely for those all-important scenes. Afterward, Al said to me, "Martin, I've never danced in a suit like the one you made for me." A terrific compliment from a terrific actor—and dancer!

Part of the challenge in making suits for movie characters involves giving the director and costume designer the look they're after while also meeting a star's individual preferences and fitting needs. In 2010, we worked with the always wonderful costume designer Juliet Polcsa to create the wardrobe for Russell Brand's character in the *Arthur* remake. The film called for Juliet to style Russell's clothes with an aristocratic Savile Row flair. Russell, however, preferred low-rise, tight, skinny pants and shrunken jackets. Our team worked hard to marry the two by creating elegant clothes that also embodied modern style notes, including custom-tailored details like working sleeve buttonholes that gave Russell the latitude to irreverently unbutton and roll up his jacket sleeves during scenes. His character also needed a jacket pocket large enough to accommodate a flask. We made all his clothes for the film save the Batman suit. Juliet received high praise from top costume designers for her work. In her gracious way, she said she "couldn't have done the film without [us]" and called our company "a national treasure."

One of the more encouraging developments in the evolution of men's fashion over the last few decades has been the elevated style with which many professional athletes now dress. Lucrative contracts, around-the-clock sports channels, endorsement deals, and a competitive drive to outshine their athletic peers have propelled today's sports stars to build serious and stylish wardrobes.

From LeBron James's teal paisley tuxedo to Kobe Bryant's ESPY Awards suits, we've hand tailored for the best. And not just basketball players. Hockey legend Wayne Gretzky, boxing great

Evander Holyfield, and my very own New York Giants' Michael
Strahan, who has made us so proud by moving from an All-Pro
football career to become a cohost on *Good Morning America*—
Martin Greenfield has dressed them all.

Dressing athletes poses several challenges, not the least of
which is that many of them are giants. But few are as large as the
seven-foot-one-inch, three-hundred-pound NBA star Shaquille
O'Neal.

We received a call from a sports agent who said one of his clients needed a suit. "I'll have him in New York. You can measure
him at the Four Seasons Hotel," the agent said.

Jay and I entered the hotel room to find the largest man I had
ever seen in my life. We had dressed the New York Knicks legend
Patrick Ewing, but Shaq made Patrick look scrawny. When I shook
Shaq's hand, I came up to his belly button. He wore a size 58 suit,
which required enough suit fabric to make a small tent. I needed a
step stool to measure him properly. When I ran my measuring tape
down the sides of his legs, I couldn't take my eyes off his feet. "My
goodness!" I said. "What size shoe do you wear?"

"I wear a size 22," he said with a giant smile.

Sometimes our Hollywood work has influenced the styles we
create for our pro athletes. Case in point: New York Knicks forward Carmelo Anthony. Carmelo, whom *Vanity Fair* has named
one of the NBA's top-ten best-dressed players, has a sophisticated
fashion sense. Not surprisingly, he likes rag & bone. Jay measured
Carmelo at the rag & bone showroom, and we've had him out to
the factory for fittings as well.

Carmelo's stylist asked me to help convince him to wear tails
to the 2014 Costume Institute Gala at the Metropolitan Museum

of Art. "Here's a picture of Steve Buscemi's character, Nucky, wearing tails on *Boardwalk Empire*. Carmelo loves that show, so maybe if you show him that picture and tell him we can do something similar, he'll go for it," she said.

I smiled so wide I could have eaten a banana sideways. "You do know that we make all the suits for *Boardwalk Empire*, right?"

Her jaw dropped. "You what?! Wait, you mean all the suits the characters wear are ones you all...."

"Every single one of them." She couldn't believe it.

When Carmelo came to the factory, I told him the old-school elegance of tails never goes out of style. "Carmelo, here's a picture of the tails I made for President Clinton," I said, handing him a photograph.

"That's real nice," he said. "But that's President Clinton. He's the president of the United States. He *has* to wear tails."

"Trust me, Carmelo. We'll do yours with a modern twist. All the clothes you love on *Boardwalk Empire*, we make those by hand. You're going to love the tails we do for you. You'll be the talk of the Met Ball." Still unsure, he trusted us enough to show him what we could do.

We made Carmelo's tails in a smart navy fabric. Just in case, Tod and Jay also suggested we have a made-to-measure navy tuxedo jacket ready in the event Carmelo didn't like the tails. In the end, though, he loved the tails. His stylist outfitted him with dapper finishes, and Carmelo ended up being one of the most stylish men at the event.

The sports world's frenetic pace forces you to get creative to find the time necessary to properly measure and fit sports figures. During our decade working with Donna Karan, Fox Football approached us about dressing all of the network's announcers, including Terry Bradshaw, John Madden, Howie Long, Pat Summerall, Jimmy Johnson, and James Brown. The producers said they would bring the whole gang together in Los Angeles for preseason preparations. We could come out then and take measurements. The session was pure insanity. Terry was being his usual joker self, Madden and Jimmy wouldn't stop yapping, and the show's producers had poor Howie on the roof of a building filming a skit while riding a motorcycle. Somehow we pulled it off and created looks each of them loved.

One of the sweetest souls in show business is Brooklyn's own Jimmy Fallon, a true-blue New Yorker and a diehard rag & bone fan to boot. My rag & bone boys, Marcus and David, introduced me to Jimmy in 2009 when he got his first gig with NBC taking over for Conan O'Brien, whom we also dressed, on the *Late Night* show.

"Jimmy," said Marcus, "I want you to meet the one and only Mr. Martin Greenfield."

"Such an honor to meet you, sir," said Jimmy. He had a sincerity and genuineness that let you know he meant it. I loved the kid the minute I met him.

"What kind of suits are your stylists putting you in right now?" I asked.

"It's a lot of Italian designer suits," said Jimmy. "They look good but the fit is so tight and uncomfortable that I can't move around on stage."

I thumbed through the rack of suits and saw all the usual labels and understood the problem immediately. I showed him a few of our rag & bone samples. He loved the shorter jackets, higher armholes, and slender lapels. "Here's what we're going to do," I told him. "I'm going to give you this rag & bone look you love but with the comfort and flexibility you need each night to do your show."

"That's awesome."

"I've seen your show. You like to jump around all over the place. You do that in those suits over there and you'll break an ankle," I joked. He laughed and said he couldn't wait to see what we could do for him.

When Jay, Joe, and I returned for the fitting a week later, Jimmy was beside himself. After trying on several of the made-to-measure rag & bone suits we made for him, he knelt on one knee and started kissing my ring. "I'm not the pope, Jimmy. I just make your suits," I said.

"To me, Mr. Greenfield, you're the pope of fashion."

When Jimmy got the call to take over for Jay Leno, he did the right thing: he brought the show back to New York like a good Brooklyn boy. He also put in an order with us for six more suits. Every time Jay and I visit him for a fitting, true to form, Jimmy kneels on one knee and kisses my ring. No ego, all class. Jimmy's going to do a beautiful job with the new gig and make Brooklyn proud.

One Brooklynite who has already made the world proud is Sir Gilbert Levine, the Jewish American conductor better known as "the pope's maestro." Levine, whose mother-in-law is an Auschwitz survivor, was the conductor of the Krakow Philharmonic in Pope John Paul II's hometown in Poland from 1987 to 1993. The pope admired his work so much that he asked him to lead the concert marking the tenth anniversary of his pontificate, as well as subsequent concerts for the church. In his wisdom, John Paul II understood how his friendship and appreciation of this Jewish American conductor could usher in a spirit of healing between Catholics and Jews around the world.

On one of his visits to the Vatican, Levine saw Cardinal Renato Raffaele Martino, who represented the Holy See in the United Nations. Each looked at the other and admired his suit. The cardinal asked the conductor, "Where did you get that suit?" Levine replied, "There is this tailor in Brooklyn...." Before he could finish, Martino opened his suit jacket and showed that he, too, was sporting a Martin Greenfield label.

In 1994, the Holy See invested Levine as a knight commander of the Order of St. Gregory the Great, the highest pontifical knighthood bestowed to a non-ecclesiastical musician since Mozart. In 2010, Pope Benedict XVI conferred on Levine the further distinction of the order's Silver Star.

I've learned in this crazy fashion business of ours to expect the unexpected. When we were asked to dress the Emmy-winning actor James Spader for NBC's *The Blacklist*, I didn't realize that my own show-biz career was about to begin. For the first season, we made twelve suits, twenty-eight vests, and thirty pants for James, who plays Raymond "Red" Reddington on the show. He and I hit it off the first time we met. His magnetic energy draws you in immediately. He and *The Blacklist* team loved the factory and the history behind it. So much so, in fact, that they filmed three scenes of the series' seventh episode, season one, at the factory.

"If we're filming at Martin Greenfield Clothiers we have to have Martin in the scene," said James.

"Me?" I said.

"Of course."

"What would I do?"

"You'd be Martin the tailor. I think you're perfect for the role, don't you?"

The scene required me to fit James's character. James is such a sweet friend that he refashioned the original script to work my name into the line so that "Red" says, "Martin, do you think the pants are too tight?" A few sharp-eyed fashion bloggers recognized my face in the scene and picked up on James's reference to "Martin." We also received several phone calls from friends, including one who informed us that *The Blacklist* "had a character on screen that looked just like Martin—and even had the same name!"

Shaping the look and styles of movie and TV characters is the professional side of the fun. Knowing about TV shows and movies before the public does excites the kid in me. Right now, for example, we're creating the looks of at least nine characters on the new Batman-based Fox TV series *Gotham*; making clothes for the Oscar Isaac and Albert Brooks movie *A Most Violent Year*; working with Steven Soderbergh on *The Knick*, a Cinemax drama set in early twentieth-century New York starring Clive Owen; and making suits for a forthcoming, as-yet-unnamed HBO rock-'n'-roll series set in the 1970s directed by Martin Scorsese and produced by Mick Jagger. We are also excited to be working with Juliet Polcsa and HBO on their project honoring the life of Joe Paterno, starring Al Pacino; and dressing Ed Burns for the show he stars in and co-produces with Steven Spielberg, *Public Morals*, a police drama set in New York City in the '60s.

In the nearly seventy years I've spent in fashion, I've never tired of the rush that comes when creative forces collide. Artists fuel artists. Helping directors, screenwriters, actors, and costume designers make their dreams and artistic visions a reality still sparks a childlike sense of wonder in me. The day that stops, so will I.

CHAPTER TWELVE

BAR MITZVAH AT EIGHTY

My life has been filled with far more light than darkness. America can do that—flood you with more blessings than you could ever deserve.

One of those blessings came Saturday, August 9, 2008. Growing up, I had never celebrated my Bar Mitzvah. By the time I was thirteen I had already fled from Pavlovo to Budapest. So when our Hampton Synagogue in Westhampton Beach told me I could celebrate my Bar Mitzvah on my eightieth birthday, I was ecstatic. Rabbi Marc Schneier would officiate. When he was thirteen years old, I made his suit for his Bar Mitzvah. Now he would be conducting mine.

In preparation for my big day, I had to learn a special *trope* (tune) to chant the *Haftarah*, a reading from the prophets that comes after the Torah reading. The *Jewish World* newspaper asked me if I was having any trouble learning the tune. It was a little tricky, I told them, but I wasn't worried about it. "If I get it wrong, what are they going to do? Shoot me?"

I could hardly wait to share the big day with my family and five hundred of our friends. When Saturday finally arrived, I wore my three-piece lavender seersucker suit. Standing before the congregation, I looked across the rows. Every face was a memory. Jay and Tod and their wives, Cheryl and Bonnie, were there, as were Arlene and my precious grandchildren, Amy, David, Sofia, and Rachel. I cried when my eyes met theirs.

Throughout the ceremony I imagined my mother, father, sisters, and baby brother looking down on me. But instead of sadness, I felt joy. When Rabbi Schneier placed the black and white striped *tallit* (prayer shawl) around me, I felt God's presence and peace.

"Here you have a survivor of the Holocaust who understands that our people's response to destruction is construction," said Rabbi Schneier. "Marty reconstructed his life. He built a successful business, and also a beautiful, loving family."

When it was my turn to speak, I told the congregation that today was a day for celebration. "Did I survive because I'm a hero? No," I said. "I survived maybe because God wanted me to survive. Or maybe I was lucky—I don't know. But I'm here. The biggest celebration of my life is today, because the odds were so against me. And I made it here, at eighty."

Only one explanation for my improbable life makes sense: God allowed America to make me possible.

I might have died a dozen times over, burned in the ovens at Auschwitz or slain at Buchenwald or some other camp, as my family and six million others were.

I might have fallen with the frozen on the Death March to Gleiwitz.

I might have been caught sneaking rations to the dying, been beaten to death, or been blown up when the bombs rained down.

I might never have found my relatives and known the joy that only family brings.

I might have wandered through life with an empty heart, never finding and marrying my dream girl.

I might never have experienced God's gift of children, wonderful sons whose hearts and talents helped build and grow my only-in-America dream.

But for some grace-filled reason, against all logic and probability, God led Americans to fight for me, to save me, to claim me as their own, to nurture me with opportunities, and to help me build a home where I could love and raise my family in my beloved Brooklyn.

I'm left with nothing but gratitude and joy for my life.

Some things, it turns out, are beyond measure.

ACKNOWLEDGMENTS

Writing a book is a little like creating a custom suit: dozens of pieces and people must all come together to help turn a vision into a seamless reality.

I want to thank Dr. Myron Finkel and Meredith McIver for helping me find Wynton Hall.

Thank you, Wynton, for helping me gather my scattered thoughts and keeping me focused. This book could not have been assembled without your laser vision and talent. Thanks also to Wynton's lovely wife, Michelle Hall, for all her valuable help and to their two precious daughters, Bella and Blakely.

And speaking of family, I of course want to thank my siblings and my parents for the values they imparted to me. Mom and Dad: I hope you are looking down with pride.

What can I say about my wife, Arlene, who has put up with me for fifty-seven years? Thank you for your love, patience, tolerance, and understanding. You have been at my side through the good and the bad. I love you more than words can express. You are my heart and my everything.

Our two sons, Jay and Tod, are *both* my right arm. My pride in them is infinite. I am lucky to have Jay's wife, Cheryl, and Tod's wife, Bonnie, as my daughters-in-law (guys, you picked well). I am happy to have their families, the Goras and the Bronszteins, as part of our family. Thank you, Paula and Jack Gora and Gilda and the late Morris Bronsztein, for the lovely gift of your daughters. Without question my grandchildren are, of course, the smartest, most beautiful grandchildren a grandfather could ever wish for. Amy, David, Rachel, and Sofia: Know that my love and pride in you are boundless. You are our family's future.

I'm grateful for Arlene's brother Kal and her mom and dad who embraced me and were always there for me.

A special thanks to all my newfound cousins in America: Frances and Moe (thank you for taking me in), Barb and Stan, Natalie and Bernie, Rikki and Louis, Joan and Lou, Ronnie, Dr. Larry and Sue, Alan and Leah, and the Gelbs and your wonderful families. I love you all.

Arlene extended my family with the addition of her cousins. Rhetta and Dr. Max and the Felton family; Judge Harold; Joseph and Francine; Gerry, Sam, and Judge Irma; Vivian; Ilene; Phyliss; Dr. Richard; Dr. Harold and Elsa; Dr. Saul and Ellen; and last but not least, Vivian, and their terrific children and grandchildren.

The Mermelsteins are like a part of my family. Kalvin was my best friend, and his brother Bennet officiated at our wedding. His brother Steve was very dear to us, as are his children Howard and

Dorothy and their families. Kalvin, I hope this book makes you smile from above, dear brother.

I also wish to recognize my GGG family. William P. Goldman of GGG was not only my mentor but my surrogate father. And Adolph Rosenberg and Sam Lipshitz provided me with support and taught me GGG's system. For that and much more, I remain forever grateful.

I want to thank Stanley Marcus of Neiman Marcus and a very special thank you to my dear, dear friend, Derrill Osborne. We love you.

I want to thank Mayor Ed Koch, who helped rebuild Brooklyn and was a great friend; Mayor Michael Bloomberg, one of our outstanding mayors; and the two greatest and best-dressed police commissioners in New York history, Ray Kelly and William Bratton.

I'm grateful for our family friends, Dr. Joe Press and Dr. Lawrence Inra, who keep me healthy and able to work six days a week. Thanks also to Fred Wilpon and Saul Katz for your forty-year friendship and the #1 Mets jacket. Being your biggest fan, I really appreciate it.

I've been blessed to work with some of the most talented professionals in the men's fashion industry, many of whom I consider friends. It's impossible to name them all, but I'd like to recognize Johnny D'Amico, Joe Gromek, Pier Guerci, Steve Grossman, Robert Kaplan, Dick Lembeck, Alan Levine, Chris Littmoden, Eric Lundgren, Aldo and Sebastiano Moscini, Nat Pittiger, Bill Roberti, Jack D. Simpson, Mickey Soloman, Walter J. Stevens, Ed Turco, Rhoda and Jack Uchitel, Dominic Verde, Eric Wilkinson, Stevie Fellig, and Steve Levitan and his family.

I especially want to thank all my hardworking and loyal employees. Your passion and dedication inspire me daily.

My spiritual mentors, Rabbis Arthur and Marc Schneier, Israel Shemtov, and Rabbi Luzer. Thank you for your prayers and wisdom throughout my long journey.

I want to thank all the wonderful friends we have made over the years, including: Bob Strauss; General Colin and Alma Powell; William T. Sullivan of the Ronald MacDonald House; Daniel Reingold with the Hebrew Home for the Aged; Marty Markowitz, former Brooklyn Borough President; Marvin Scott; Al Shragis; Tom Clancy; Bruce Llewellyn; Mike Rotchford and Charlotte Kolb; Judge Roz Mauskopf and family; Cardinal Edward Egan; Sir Gilbert Levine; Ron Perelman; and Maurice R. Greenberg.

A special thanks to all my friends who have stuck with us over the years. We love you all. Magda Silberman, Judy and Harry Goldstein, the Heller families, the Berebichez family (Oh, those Acapulco years!), Pam and Mark Rubin, Miriam Silverman, Marcy Brown, Sandy and Artie Rosenbluth, Marcia and Michael Cherbini, and last, but not least, the old Brooklyn friends: Edie and Bob Wallach, the Katz family, Sheila and Stan Josephson, Iris and Donald Seckendorf, Linda and Bob Siegfeld, and the two who have stuck the longest, Norma and Richard Berlin and their families and the newcomers, Marlene and Marty Jacobson.

I am grateful to the brilliant and talented roster of world-class designers and industry greats we've had the pleasure of working with through the years: Donna Karan, Alexander Julian (I'll always be honored to be called your "maker"), Calvin Klein, Perry Ellis, Isaac Mizrahi, Scott Sternberg of Band of Outsiders, the rag & bone dynamic duo of Marcus Wainwright and David Neville, and several more.

I also wish to thank the talented and dedicated team at Regnery: publisher Marji Ross, editor Tom Spence, Harry Crocker, and the entire publicity team. Thanks also to Patrick Smith of Wynton Hall & Co. and to my New York City literary agent Glen Hartley at Writers' Reps for his passion and belief in this project.

Finally, Martin Greenfield Clothiers would like to extend a warm thank-you to all the celebrities we have had the privilege of working alongside and dressing through the years: Presidents Dwight D. Eisenhower, Gerald Ford, Bill Clinton, and Barack Obama; Vice President Joe Biden; Senator Bob Dole; Secretary Donald Rumsfeld; Sammy Davis Jr.; Frank Sinatra; Dean Martin; Jerry Lewis; Michael Jackson; Martin Scorsese; Terence Winter; Baz Luhrmann; Catherine Martin; Steven Soderbergh; Jimmy Fallon; Denzel Washington; Leonardo DiCaprio; Tobey Maguire; Johnny Depp; Ben Affleck; Steve Buscemi; James Spader; Donald Trump; Walter Cronkite; Stone Phillips; Michael Strahan; LeBron James; Shaquille O'Neal; Patrick Ewing; Carmelo Anthony; Kobe Bryant; John Cusack; Conan O'Brien; Jonah Hill; Clive Owen; Kanye West; Joel Edgerton; Eddie Cantor; Ben Stiller; Sir Ben Kingsley; Matt Czuchry; Michael Shannon; Oscar Issac; Kevin Bacon; Paul Newman; Al Pacino; Michael Douglas; Ellen Miro-jnick; John Dunn; Bobby Cannavale; Vincent Piazza; Michael Stuhlbarg; Michael K. Williams; Stephen Graham; Dabney Coleman; Michael Pitt; Raúl Esparza; Richard Belzer; André Holland; Alan Alda; and many, many more.

INDEX